HOME IMPROVEMENT SURVIVAL GUIDE FOR MEN

Miles,
Stop looking at this book and get on with the job!

Good luck, I'm sure you'll nail it,

Paul, Claire Adam & Ben
x

HOME IMPROVEMENT SURVIVAL GUIDE FOR MEN

Dan Van Oss

Copyright © 2015 Dan Van Oss

All rights reserved.

Contents

BEFORE WE START
Home Improvement Throughout History 16
(Mrs. Lorenzo de Medici and the Metric Death Star)
Saving Your Marriage 20
(Kiwi Sunset vs. the ZZ Top Guest Toilet)
Should you hire a professional? 23
(Wife: YES!)
Basic Tools 27
(Hairy Karl Hates Your Girly Man Gloves)
Understanding Dimensions & Measurements 32
(Ted the Paint Man and The Board from the Nominal Dimension)

WIRING AND ELECTRICAL
Wiring & Electrical Basics 36
Project: Replacing a Light Fixture 41
Tip Time: Stripping wire 46
Project: Installing a Dimmer Switch 49
Electrical Energy Savers 54

PLUMBING
Plumbing Basics 60
Project: Fixing a Leaky Faucet 62
Tip Time: Soldering Copper Pipe 66
Project: Unclogging a Drain 69
Project: Replacing a Toilet 73

INDOOR PROJECTS
Project: Build a Saw Horse 80
Project: Painting a Room 83
Project: Wallpapering a Room 87
Tip Time: Wall Anchors: The Hardware Industry's Way of Giving You An In-Home Mental Health Assessment 90
Project: Installing a New Towel Bar 96
Project: Hanging the Perfect Picture 102
Tip Time: Pulling nails 106
Project: Fixing Squeaks 108
Project: Drywall Repair 112

OUTDOOR PROJECTS
Tip Time: Renting Tools 118
Project: Putting in a New Mailbox 122
Project: Building a Wooden Fence 127
Tip Time: Freeing Stuck Nuts, Bolts and Screws 132
Project: Cutting Down a Tree 135
Project: Planting a Tree 139
Project: Pest Protection (No, Sweetheart, I'm Not Killing Mickey, It's Vermin) 143

Home Improvement Glossary 147
Home Improvement Haikus 157
Epilogue 159
Thanks for Reading! 163
About the Author 164

Obligatory Disclaimer (i.e., Don't Sue Me)

If I had a lawyer, this is probably the part where he or she would tell me to definitely let you know that I'm not responsible for any death, dismemberment, unintentional hilarity, electrocution, verbal spousal abuse, or neighborhood public humiliation that may occur by following any of the tips or projects in this guide. It is not intended to be taken too seriously, unless serious things are what make you laugh, in which case, have at it. Seriously.

Preface

This book is for all guys who are expected, just because they have a Y chromosome, to know how to fix a running toilet, a stopped toilet, or a toilet that has just plain given up on life because, well, it's a toilet. You're also supposed to know how to build functional yet beautiful lawn furniture out of scraps left over from your kid's science fair medieval catapult project, or how to repair a lawn mower that just started puking smoke like some weekend-regretting robotic frat boy. But just because we're guys doesn't mean we're inherently handy, as is evidenced by that unfixed weed whacker with it's intestines spilled onto the floor that you keep tripping over in your garage. That's like assuming that all women know how to bake a cake, or all dogs know how to poop outside. On the contrary, most guys have had a fair share of home improvement mishaps, along with the medical bills and ruined shirts to prove it. This book is full of advice that your average Joe can relate to, even if his name is not Joe, and is not meant for guys who can build a hurricane-proof, gingerbread-trimmed utility shed in a weekend with their heavily-muscled construction buddies who like to wear flannel shirts with the sleeves ripped off. It is not for the inordinately-testosteroned guys who have perfect, clean pickups with those diamond-patterned chrome tool boxes, whose first words as a baby were "nail gun" or "hack saw". This is for you: the guy who has trouble getting the twist tie off a bag of cheese curds; who learned how to properly fall off a ladder from his dad, who in turn learned how to fall off a ladder from *his* dad, all the way back to your great-great-great-great-grandfather, who was a deck hand on Columbus's boat, and fell out of the crows nest when he was trying to install the motion detecting light his wife wanted because she thought she saw a stranger on deck the other night.

We'll look at some skills that can help you at least appear to be competent when your father-in-law, who worked something like 45 years as Chief Engineer on the starship *Enterprise* and can build a working light bulb from a Coke bottle and a gum wrapper, comes to visit at Christmas. And I'll show you step-by-step instructions to a few common projects you'll encounter around your house, provided it hasn't vibrated it to the ground already after last weeks' ceiling fan installation debacle. Now, let's get started on the long, dusty, rusty-nail-sticking-out-of-the-board-and-poking-into-your-foot-because-you-forgot-to-wear-your-boots-like-your-wife-told-you-to-but-no-way-are-you-ever-going-to-tell-her-THIS-happened road of home improvement success.

PART ONE: BEFORE WE START

Where's the Nearest Emergency Room, Again?

Home Improvement Throughout History (Mrs. Lorenzo de Medici and the Metric Death Star)

THE INABILITY TO INSTINCTIVELY KNOW HOW to fix or build stuff, as with most things involving the shortcomings of males, is nothing new to history. You might think you're the only guy who's ever had to slink into a hardware store and ask why the light-activated nightlight you just bought won't stay on during the daytime, but rest assured, a similar doofus as far back as prehistory has had to bring back the set of rocks he bought at Cronk's Cave Improvement Hut because he needed <u>metric</u> pebbles to fix his Japanese-made club. In fact, history is loaded with examples from art and literature of inept or browbeaten guys trying to fix or build stuff, such as:

- Cave murals depicting various men futilely trying to hang a Thomas Kinkade painting in solid rock using a mastodon jaw and sharp sticks.
- Egyptian pottery art showing a woman bearing a distinct look of irritation while watching her husband struggling to change a chariot wheel.
- An account from the poem "Sir Gawain and

The Green Knight" where: "Gawain gripped his axe and glanced it on high, his left foot on the field before him he set, slipped then on the screwdriver had left he on the garage floor, the fraught of which his maiden had warned, roughly he reached out, to no avail, his golden locks concussed, thus pined he for an ice pack from the freezer."

- Rare lithograph of Michelangelo being forced to repaint a kitchen because Mrs. Lorenzo de Medici didn't like Burnt Avocado Green.
- A motet by Mozart entitled "Postríduo Applica Scandere Poli," which, roughly translated, means, "Wench, Bring the Ladder; It Tumbled Prostrate When I Was On The Roof Putting Up The Christmas Lights."
- A recently discovered 18th-century painting of Simón Bolívar trying to fix a toaster with a fork.
- A 20th-century cubist painting of a man falling down the stairs after tripping on an extension cord he was going to wrap later.
- And so on.

It may help to remind yourself that life, as you should know if you survived junior high school, is imperfect. Why, even the earth itself wobbles on its axis, so how can you be expected to keep your newly installed ceiling fan from shimmying like an epileptic belly dancer? Nature abhors a vacuum, especially the one that you're going to need to clean up the broken glass from that dropped fluorescent light tube. And electricity, water pressure, gravity, inertia, credit debt, original sin, and other immense, immutable forces are, by their nature, rooting for your failure. You must be the do-it-yourself Luke Skywalker against the home improvement Death Star, except your light saber is a cracked cordless drill and a cheap American socket set, and the Death Star's thermal exhaust port has metric bolts.

Many of you learned your home improvement skills from your father or grandfathers and still use some of their tools, complete with familiar paint spatters, gouges from drops on concrete, and the occasional faded blood smear. I know I learned many helpful skills from my dad, such as how to drill through a board into your index finger, how to run upstairs in 2.3 seconds to put your hand in ice after grabbing the wrong end of a soldering iron, or how to not tell mom where the new hole in her favorite tablecloth came from. These are prototypical man things and should be embraced and honored. There should be memorials and statues in every town square to all of the guys before us who built crooked fences and dropped paint cans upside down onto the floor. Granted, these statues would most likely be erected by men and so would themselves be crooked and falling apart, because someone decided using duct tape was good enough for now, plus they had bowling league to get to. But that would be the ironic beauty of it. So, I say we embrace our undeniable mediocrity without shame, knowing we are just trying to make the world better, one fried circuit breaker and flooded bathroom at a time.

So, even though the odds are stacked against you historically (and possibly genetically), there's still time to save some face, or at least some shin or knuckle skin, during your home improvement tenure on earth. Just because your last project involved three firemen and a cease-and-desist order from the nearby hardware store doesn't mean you can't now learn how to install a simple dimmer switch in your bathroom without taking down your local power grid. Just remember, there are plenty of ice packs and band-aids for all of us.

Saving Your Marriage (Kiwi Sunset vs. the ZZ Top Guest Toilet)

THIS SECTION IS FOR YOU GUYS who are in the midst of having to install giant, flowered, pillowcase-matching window treatments on a beautiful Saturday afternoon when you can see your neighbor cheerfully driving away with his golf clubs in the back of his truck. I'm going to assume you're married, because a) a single guy wouldn't care whether his window treatments match his pillowcases, which naturally heighten the ambience of the room, b) a single guy doesn't even know what "window treatments" are, only has one <u>Dukes of Hazard</u> pillowcase he's had since third grade, and thinks "ambience" is a Dallas Cowboys cheerleader, and c) the only reason you have this book is because your wife bought it after your last project, which left your dog and one of your children with a (temporary?) pink streak in their fur/hair.

Men, never start any project without first consulting your wife. A wife can start any project she wants without too much fear of retribution, because she can always cry and make you feel horrible, whereas a guy crying because he installed a surge protector backwards and burnt out his new 65" TV is just pathetic and embarrassing. Your wife will have many useful and probably well-worn pieces of advice for you, mostly involving not having things happen, such as electrocution, dismemberment, unintentional holes, or really anything involving blood or an inch of water on the kitchen floor. So, as much as you might think you were born with a green thumb and can handle any project, you need to realize that you probably don't know everything, especially the part about green thumbs having to do with gardening and not home repair.

When you are discussing a project with your spouse that you really want to do because you saw it on <u>Freddy's Fix-It</u> show on public access TV during a baseball game rain delay, and it only took him 22 minutes to build, and it had a built-in refrigerator and everything, make sure to use calming, non-technical terms and phrases, such as "cheap" or "spackle will fix that." Point out all of the features and benefits of your new project, such as enhanced home value, or extra light, or finally being able to prove to your father-in-law that you weren't just bragging about knowing how to wield a sawzall in a lift bucket. You should also be on the same page about colors, designs, and, most importantly, cost before proceeding, as many a divorce arbitrator has had to sadly shake his head when hearing, yet again, how "someone WOULD appreciate a $399 custom ZZ Top guest toilet if someone KNEW how much SOMEONE ELSE always LOVED ZZ Top!"

You don't want to be in the middle of a project arguing about whether the new "Kiwi Sunset" kitchen paint color looked more bluish-green than greenish-blue in the store, especially while the workers are standing around wondering if maybe they should have chosen a different profession, such as bull riding, or being the guy who operates the machine they use to give people electro shock treatments. Your contractor won't care whether one of you thinks the new bathroom tile looks like the cat puked up spoiled guacamole, as they have probably not gone to psychotherapy school and will get paid the same regardless.

I suggest, by way of totally stealing the idea from someone else, that you make a list of things you each Absolutely Must Have, things you Would Like To Have If Possible, things that are Totally Optional, and Things That Will Make Divorce A Distinct Possibility If They Are Implemented In My House. Try to keep your remodeling ideas located in List One as much as possible, or, if you're feeling particularly antagonistic because of the ZZ Top toilet thing, you could shoot the moon and go for everything in List Four, in which case you will soon have the whole house to yourself, and can bask in your loneliness sitting on your sofa with the built-in cat habitrail you demanded, having won the battle over friezé or loop pile carpet.

Should you hire a professional? (Wife: YES!)

DO YOU REMEMBER WHEN YOU READ THAT ARTICLE about "10 Steps to Better Curb Appeal" in the home improvement magazine in the doctor's office waiting to be seen for a possible broken finger as a result of using your cordless drill to make homemade ice cream because the ice cream maker wasn't working because you had the bright idea once to use it for mixing plaster to fix the hole you made in the entryway wall when you were chasing the dog because he knocked over the open paint can you were using to paint the front door to give it more curb appeal, and you thought, "I should probably finish that project..."? You might consider hiring a professional. [Wife: YES!]

Professionals are paid for a reason: they have spent years collecting the right tools and acquiring the needed skills for accomplishing each job, and have learned, through constant practice, how not to laugh in your face when they find out that the reason your refrigerator isn't working is that you mistakenly unplugged *it* instead of the toaster oven, which you had to take outside because it was smoking from the pepperoni pizza rolls you left on at 400 degrees and forgot about because there was a special on Michael

Jordan on ESPN you had only seen two times. Yes, professionals cost money, but just like many other preventative measures, such as home accident insurance or unlimited shopping credit for your wife, they are sometimes worth it.

Question 1: How risky is it?
The Greek philosopher Sophocles once said, "The dice of Zeus always fall lucky." I'm going to go with the odds here and assume your name isn't Zeus, which means your dice are about as lucky as mine, which is to say, not at all. So, when considering whether to proceed with a project, does it involve:

a) The removal of live animals with teeth and/or stingers?
b) Heights greater than you can safely fall without having your wife look at you like she did when you dropped the hammer and cracked the tile floor when you were pretending you were Thor and the coat rack was Loki?
c) Moving objects heavier than your old college hide-a-bed that you tried hauling down to the basement yourself and ended up giving the cat an unfortunate lesson in mass and inertia?
d) Indoor water?
e) Physics?
f) Invisible forces such as electricity, wind, or perpetual shame?

You might consider hiring a professional.

Question 2: Will it be worth your time?
The wise home improvement maestro will carefully

balance the time and effort it will take to finish a particular project with the amount of money his wife says he will have available after he finishes buying her the anniversary present he forgot to buy last week. Sure, it will take three long weekends doing what would take a professional 3 hours to do, but that joker wants 400 bucks, and you can't see how he's going to be able to patch the hardwood hallway floor where you dropped the bowling ball any better than you can. Better to save that money to fix the bend in the garage door track you banged into two winters ago when you tried putting skis on the riding lawn mower so you could give rides to the neighbor kids. Also, there is (unfortunately) no statute of limitations on home improvement, so you don't want to be that guy in the neighborhood who has had about 5 ongoing projects for the past three years, each with various pieces sticking out of the ground covered with blue tarps. You should know that "home improvement completion time" is like "time it takes for the traffic light to change when I really need to get to a bathroom time"; twice as long and always with the potential for an unwanted accident.

Question 3: Do you have the knowledge or skills to accomplish the task?

Just as many guys think they are really good looking, even though their hair is no longer in the same decade as they are and they weigh more than all of their children combined, you may also think you possess handyman abilities far beyond your skill level. Just because you helped your neighbor Jim, who builds things out of concrete for a living, hold a board for 3 minutes while he installed an in-ground swimming pool with a minibar doesn't mean you now possess the knowledge to construct a patio that doesn't look like a T-Rex angrily took a squat on it. Your grandfather may have been a brilliant carpenter, but the human genome project has not yet found the allele for Dremel tool skill, so don't be surprised when you start running out of band-aids. As always, if you are uncertain whether you should proceed with a project because of a lack of skill, ask your wife; she will be happy to give you an honest, forthright, and quite possibly loud opinion. If you are unmarried, go for it - what have you got to lose?

Question 4: Do you like watching sports on weekend afternoons?

You should hire a professional.

Basic Tools (Hairy Karl Hates Your Girly Man Gloves)

HIRING A PROFESSIONAL IS ONE WAY TO HOME IMPROVEMENT NIRVANA; actually, it's probably the only way. However, we know some of you want to experience the thrill of "having done it all myself" and "knowing the fastest way to the emergency room." So, if you're going to be a well-respected home fixit guy, you're going to need some basic tools, because you can't just keep going over to your neighbor Steve to borrow his; remember, you still have the grass trimmer he loaned you last summer.

Gloves
Hand protection is essential for many home-improvement projects, and a good pair of gloves can provide you up to two days earlier release out of the hospital after your accident. Choosing the correct gloves, however, is imperative. Don't end up borrowing your wife's floral-print cotton gardening gloves and run the risk of being seen by your hairy Ukrainian neighbor Karl out walking his dog, who will flat-out call you a "Divchatka Lyudyna" (girly man) to your face while shaking his head. You need manly gloves, preferably made out of mastodon hide, or some other especially testosterone-laden material, so

that when you drop that 80-pound retaining wall block on your toe, you can blame it on "these new gloves." These days, because we Americans are ridiculously excessive in everything (see "lawn mower racing," "triple-ply toilet paper," etc.), you can get gloves for almost any work situation. Fingerless gloves for better dexterity and potential thumb slicing; stiff, high-impact gloves for maximum dropping of that screw you need that just slipped down the funnel while you were changing your car's oil; all-leather black gloves, which double well when you need that last-minute Batman costume at Halloween; or fire-retardant gloves to help you get the screwdriver out of the grill that you dropped when you were trying to fix the broken flame adjuster you should have repaired last spring. Your gloves will become your most familiar tool and provide many memories of past projects by way of oil, paint, and eventually, blood stains.

Utility Knife
Before you can start most home-improvement projects, you'll usually need to open at least one American Psychiatric Association of Deranged Ex-Practitioner-approved supremely irritating plastic clamshell packaged item designed to drive even Mahatma Gandhi to want to smack his mother in the face. This is the unopenable packaging that proves man is sinful and in need of salvation, as no sane person would design this except to torture his fellow human beings. Something as simple as wanting to open a new toy for your baby becomes a tortuous, finger-slicing lesson in new and unusual curse words and the depravity of man. This is where your trusty

utility knife comes in, allowing you to safely open the offending package while, at the same time, cutting the bejeepers out of your countertop. Your standard utility knife usually contains a secret compartment where the extra blades hang out, which no one tells you about because they figure every guy is supposed to have been born with this information, just like we're inherently supposed to know how to connect jumper cables. You don't want to use too many of these blades, as they cost money, so make sure you use the same, dull blade for about 2 years before changing it, finally giving in when you can't even open an envelope with it anymore. It also makes a great doorstop, fingernail cleaner, letter opener, and screwdriver after you've broken the tip off trying to use it to open a paint can.

Cordless Drill
If Michelangelo had had a cordless drill he could have completed his statue of David in about 3 days. Granted, it would have looked liked a third grader's marble rendition of Elmer Fudd, but he would at least have had some extra time for back therapy after painting that Sistine Chapel thing. The modern cordless drill has better battery life and more torque than your grandfather's version, which was one of those twisty ones that took both hands to use and couldn't drill anything much smaller than a porthole on a sailboat. The current move toward lithium batteries has produced a longer-lasting, much more relaxed drill that is less susceptible to mood swings. You'll want to keep two batteries on hand: one in the drill and one on the charger you forgot to plug in, so that you have an excuse to take nice, two-hour

inconsequential sporting event viewing breaks between charges.

Tape Measure
Experienced home improvers keep this tool with them at all times, as you'll never know when you'll need to delude someone with the idea that you have real handyman prowess. Experts prefer the wide, 25-foot long tapes, because they don't bend when measuring long distances and are the most fun to painfully snap back into your buddy's hand when they least expect it.

Level
You'll be using this tool more than you think, as it is essential for aligning anything that requires more than one hole, such as pictures, shelves, ledges, racks, towel bars, or golf courses. Also doubles as a straight edge, doorstop, curious dog whacker, ineffective pry bar, worthless hammer, and, when accidentally dropped, unexpected paint stirrer.

Tool Carrier
Nothing says "I'm a man" like getting a testicular check at your yearly physical. But that's probably for another book. What we're talking about here is the one necessary element for all serious home-improvement enthusiasts, and maybe even for you semi-serious ones, or you guys that just keep laughing as you pound away at everything. The tool box of yesteryear, with its quaint compartments where your granddad would keep his pipe tobacco, square nails, awls, plumb bobs, and what not has given way to the modern tool carrier, which can house up to 50 fighter aircraft, achieve speeds of 30 knots, and has

displacements of up to 45,000 tons in full battle mode. You'll want to keep the tool carrier near you on all projects, as you'll never know when you're going to want to change the station on its built-in FM radio, because you really hate that one Def Leppard song about sugar.

Understanding Dimensions & Measurements (Ted the Paint Man and The Board from the Nominal Dimension)

WHEN I WAS GROWING UP, we not only lived under the threat of imminent nuclear war with the Soviet Union, but were also constantly warned to expect, at any time, probably during the night when we were sleeping and one of the doors had been foolishly left unlocked, the Metric System to arrive. Get ready, they said, for when your children are grown, you'll need to be able tell them how much oxygen to add to your bedside Digital Lung and what size Dinner Pill to stick in your feeding tube, and it will be in metric, and you won't know what to ask for, and you'll asphyxiate or starve. So we waited, and put milliliter measurements in tiny numbers on our pork and beans cans next to the ounces, and tried to remember whether a centimeter was bigger than a hectare, or if zero degrees centigrade was how cold it was in space or whether we could still go outside without a hat.

We're still waiting, and that's why, when working with many home-improvement projects, you will run up against traditional, fractional math so complex you'd steal the wheels off Stephen Hawking's wheelchair just to know whether the board you're cutting to build the scooter ramp for your overweight mother-in-law is too short, or whether you're turning it into fresh scrap wood because you calculated it 12 millimeters — excuse me — 1/8 of an inch too short.

One of the main confusions is a result of lumberyards using "nominal" and "actual" dimensions, a system, which, if used by, say, plastic surgeons, would result in a lot of people having one leg shorter than the other, or hairlines that started at the back of the head. For example, when you pick up a 2 x 4 at your local Home Improvement Depository, you are not getting a board that measures 2 inches by 4 inches, but 1-1/2 inches by 3-1/2 inches (or 38 mm × 89 mm if you're British or me in math class in the 70s). How did this come to be? Should we call Geraldo for a feverish exposé on the duplicitous lumber industry? Well, nominal dimensions were historically the size of the rough, un-dried (or green) lumber; however, when it is dried and planed, it becomes self-conscious and shrinks. The lumber industry, which is either as lazy or as horrible with numbers as I am, has decided to keep the system in its current confusing state, possibly because they're still expecting us to someday actually switch to the metric system, and so are avoiding having to reprint all of their lumber dimension calendars with the pictures of happy beavers in overalls building a birdhouse they give out free at the hardware store while you're waiting for Ted the paint man to mix the wrong color of "Tickled Bunny Lavender" for your kitchen.

PART TWO: WIRING AND ELECTRICAL
Frankenstein's Monster Was Right To Be Angry

Wiring & Electrical Basics

THERE'S NOTHING QUITE LIKE THE FEELING of completing a practical, home-enhancing electrical project, unless it's the mind-numbing buzzing you're still recovering from because you forgot to turn off the breaker to the outlet you were working on, again. So be warned: electricity, while providing us with many modern home conveniences such as egg steamers, classic vibrating football games, and electric bills, is quite capable of sending you a very specific message, which is, usually, "You were really dumb to touch that." But not to worry; about 80% of the time, you can fix about 25% of a quarter of most of your electrical problems in less than 15 minutes.

As with all electrical projects in this book, great care must be taken not to sue me if you screw it up, because I can't be expected to know everything, and I've got my own electrical issues to worry about, okay? So, before you start any project, your first step will always be to make sure the electricity to the circuit you are working on has been disabled. To do this, you'll either be working with a circuit breaker box or a fuse box or, in extremely screwed up houses, a circuit box with fuse breakers.

Circuit Breakers and Fuse Boxes
If you have a circuit breaker box, you'll need to check

the dusty, faded list of labels loosely pasted inside that look like they were written by a dyslexic partridge to see if there is a circuit labeled, say, anything remotely like "Kitchen Lights" or "Garage Outlets." Usually, you'll have to sift through cryptic abbreviations such as "Nrt Basmnt Flunge," "Hallwy Circ w/Scenic Bypass," or "3-Prong BWX Rcon Snrt," etc. Some of these aren't actually connected to anything; they're just there to make electricians feel like they're really smart compared to you. Next, you might want to enlist the help of a family member, preferably one who doesn't think you're just about to kill yourself with 10,000 volts, which is to say, not your wife. Have the light you intend to work on switched on, or, if you're working on an outlet, plug a light into it, and as you try turning off breakers to the various, incomprehensibly labeled switches, have your teenager yell out "It's off!" – unless they get distracted by a text message telling them the party is at Jeremy's tonight, but Becky is going to be there OMG who invited HER, in which case, you've got some yelling of your own to do.

If you're working on an electrical outlet, here's an old electrician's trick for when you're working alone or just don't want anybody's help because you're a grown man and can do it by yourself. Plug a radio into the outlet, tune it to the oldies station, and turn it up loud enough so you can hear "Takin' Care of Business" by Bachmann-Turner Overdrive from the circuit breaker box. This is for two reasons: 1) when you turn off the correct breaker, the sound will disappear, and you'll know you have the right one, and 2) really annoying your teenager who didn't want to help you at all and who now has to listen to Billy Idol sing "White Wedding" at full volume.

If your house uses fuses, it's really old, and you should consult that scene in <u>A Christmas Story</u> where the Old Man is plugging the leg lamp into an octopus of extension cords and there are sparks and the fuse goes out, and he has to go down into the basement to curse. That's pretty much what's in store for you.

Note: If you have aluminum wiring, which is a dull gray color, call in a professional, because some hippie electrical contractor wired your house with extruded recycled beer cans.

Wire Gauges
Here's a list of the various sizes or "gauges" of wire, along with their general uses, that you may encounter during your tribulation as a surrogate electrician.

16 Gauge
Don't worry about gauges this size or smaller; it's either in stuff so small you should probably just buy a new one instead of trying to fix it, or so intricate you'll feel like you're trying to defuse a bomb and end up having an anxiety attack.

14 Gauge
You'd think because this number is lower that the wire would be thicker than 16 gauge, but it's not. That's just another way electricity tries to mess with your head. Anyway, this is the gauge you'll probably be working with the most, as it is most commonly found in light switches, electrical boxes, or whatever else it is you blew up trying to dry the

dog with a leaf blower.
12 Gauge
This is the most common of the smoothbore firearms, comprising up to 50% of the shotgun mark... uh, wait, hang on; I Googled the wrong thing again... Okay, here we go. This gauge is used primarily for laundry, small appliances, and bathroom circuits – areas of the house which you should be leery of because they combine water and electricity, and if my 5th grade science teacher Mr. Snorgenson (who couldn't feel anything in his left hand because of what he would only say was a botched shower radio installation) can be trusted, that's not good.
10 Gauge
Used for larger appliances, such as washing machines, refrigerators, domestic robots, those vibrating beds they used to have in motels – pretty much anything electrical you can't lift on your own, even if you wanted to.
8 Gauge
This is Big Boy wiring for houses, apartment buildings, and factories – anything that is basically rectangular, immobile, and needs lots of electricity. If you're seeing this gauge, you've either had an earthquake or a sci-fi monster attack and so have bigger problems to deal with.
6 Gauge
This gauge is for "feeder" wire, which I'm going to assume has nothing to do with a cool electronic gadget you can get from Hammacher Schlemmer like a voice-activated Doritos-fetching machine.
1/0 Gauge
This is the size of wire they use on power stations

with the signs on the chain link fences that say WARNING with the picture of the clumsy guy being zapped across the universe by angry, red electrical bolts. If you encounter this, you either work for the power company or have had an unfortunate hot air balloon accident, or both.

3/0 Gauge
Cable used on the Golden Gate Bridge, and possibly to feed Electro's secret lair.

Project: Replacing a Light Fixture

TO HELP SET UP THIS NEXT PROJECT, you need to picture that one scene in that Bruce Lee movie; I think it was <u>Fists or Abs or Dragons of Fury</u>, or maybe it was <u>Return of the Fists or Abs or Dragons of Fury</u>; anyway, someone was really furious. So, Bruce Lee goes to the bad guy's office and, just to show everyone how unbelievably tough he is, kicks out the ceiling light from where he's standing, while the guy who was going to attack him looks like he just had a spontaneous bodily fluid evacuation he hadn't experienced since he was a baby. Now, just imagine that's what broke your ceiling light instead of the pool cue you were twirling because you were trying to impress your kids with your Tom Cruise <u>Color of Money</u> reenactment, which they would never have gotten the reference to anyway as they weren't even born when the movie came out.

But don't worry; replacing a light fixture need not be a difficult or expensive job, although, considering the fact that you're cleaning Tom Cruise-induced glass shards out of your rec room carpet, it probably will be both. But let's do our best to think positively, because that seems to work for Disney characters, and I don't think I've ever seen one of them fall off a ladder because they stepped on a loose screwdriver while putting up a wall sconce, except maybe Goofy. Once again, it is worth noting that electricity, just like intestinal viruses, may be invisible, but it can embarrass you at the most inopportune times, so be careful.

Recommended Tools:
- Hammer
- Cordless drill
- Cordless drill with actual charged battery
- Wire stripper
- Wire cutters
- Wire connectors
- Wire
- Old, rickety ladder you got at your ex-neighbor's garage sale because you felt sorry for them and it was only 5 bucks
- Dorky headlamp that makes you look like the world's most inept spelunker

First, you must choose a new fixture. You may have your heart set on that chandelier of upside-down Chicago Bears football helmets with the light bulbs that look like Walter Payton, but I would suggest opting for something more conservative and less practically insane. Make sure your ceiling can handle any extra weight your new fixture may have, as you don't want to have an impromptu re-enactment of the chandelier falling scene from <u>Phantom of The Opera</u> when your boss is over for dinner.

1) Switch off the breaker in your junction box (See Previous Chapter). Note: even if you've

switched off the correct breaker, you could still get shocked. How? Well, your daughter could come in the room and tell you she's decided to accept an invitation to take a spontaneous trip to the El Salvador rainforest with a guy she just met in art class who calls himself "Shugg" and paints upside-down portraits of the Jolly Green Giant on papyrus as a protest against Whole Foods no longer carrying carbon-neutral quinoa. Or your teenage son could announce that he's decided that hanging up wet towels is a really swell idea. Or, less frighteningly, the junction box you are working on could contain wiring from multiple circuits, some of which you might find are still live, and so may proceed to try to make you feel quite the opposite. Electrical contractors will occasionally do this because they have private deals with local hospitals, where they get secret kickbacks from the ER visits of unsuspecting do-it-yourself morons. To avoid this, I recommend using a technique I call "abject, sweaty fear," which involves using a tool I never heard of before called a "noncontact voltage tester." Use this tool to poke around the box to see if any other circuits are still active, all the while wondering if this device really works or if the manufacturer is taking a percentage from the aforementioned electrical contractors' hospital scam.

2) Using your rickety, second-hand ladder, remove the old fixture by using a series of grunts and sub-breath mutterings, and possibly a screwdriver. Note that for many of you,

removing the old fixture is an easy process because half of it is already missing from whatever accident precipitated the need for this project (see "Tom Cruise," above).
3) Make sure you don't reuse the old wire connectors from the previous connections because you got new ones in the packaging of your new fixture, and they're cooler because they're blue.
4) If your current junction box is recessed more than a 1/4 inch from the surface of the ceiling, you have a code violation, and swarms of Kevlar-armored tactical electricians will drop from black utility company helicopters on zip lines and smash through your windows and proceed to haul you off to electrical jail, where you will be tormented by angry guards with cattle prods dressed as Reddy Kilowatt. To avoid this, you'll need to use a box extender, which you can pick up anywhere that sells box extenders, which is to say you'll have to order it online.
5) Secure your new fixture to the electrical box using the supplied hardware, and, if necessary, an oath about the suspicious genealogy of the designer of "prevailing torque lock" nuts. You'll quickly find that the main challenge of working on a new ceiling fixture will come in the form of gravity, which you should be familiar with because it is the same force that has probably precipitated most of your trips to the emergency room. Trying to hang a heavy fixture while simultaneously holding a screwdriver and some twist connectors and

balancing on a rickety, half-broken ladder will make you feel like a member of Cirque du Soleil, except you're the member that hands out the programs and not the one that is spinning plates while dancing on top of a flaming elephant. Using a piece of heavy wire to suspend the fixture from the junction box while you're making the electrical connections is a handy trick, or, if you have some skills in quantum mechanics and general relativity theory, you could first try to build a Gravity Well Inversion Remodulator, and then just do everything upside down.

6) A common challenge when working on anything linking electricity and light is that without the one you don't have the other. Which means that that bright, helpful overhead light you're going to work on isn't going to give you any bright, helpful overhead light while you're working on it. This is where one of those LED headlamps comes in handy because it not only gives bright, directional light while you're working, it also makes you look like a total dork. But since you'll be working in your own house with your own family, I suspect this will be very familiar ground.

Your new fixture should now be ready to give you years of bright, cheery light, provided you didn't go ahead and install that Chicago Bears chandelier, in which case your joy will be short-lived because your wife is warming up for her own Tom Cruise <u>The Color of Money</u> reenactment.

Tip Time: Stripping wire

SECURE, STRONG ELECTRICAL CONNECTIONS always begin with neat and accurate writing down of the electrician's phone number in case things go south. After that, you'll need some wire, which, in the case of most electrical projects, is ridiculously abundant. However, in order to make these connections and complete your project so you can get back to your Netflix <u>Cheers</u> marathon, you'll need to cleanly strip the insulation from the wire.

First, you need to score the jacket. This is not an obscure high school drug reference but refers to cutting away the outer sleeve of the cable that houses the internal wires. This is best done skillfully, but there is, as always, another way that I prefer. It involves using your utility knife [insert wife suddenly looking up in fear here] and your big thumb [sound of wife frantically putting emergency room phone number as a predial on her cell phone]. Cut gently around the outer sheath with the knife on one side and your thumb on the other, slowly rotating until you have either cut through the outer sheath or your thumb. If it's your thumb, that's why God made super glue, so tell your wife to chill out and put down the phone.

Next, we need to remove the protective plastic

covering the internal wires. Now, I grew up stripping wires the old-fashioned way: using an old, dull knife I got from my grandfather's toolkit that even he couldn't get sharp anymore, and using it to mercilessly gnaw at the wire until I had removed too much insulation and had to start the process all over. A much better way is to use a wire stripping tool, which looks like an extra part that fell off C3PO and has various notches and guides which are great for nonchalantly showing your neighbor Steve as evidence that you really know what you're doing, even though he can clearly see you're holding it upside down. The notches fit various gauges of wire, which, even though you've probably already forgotten what gauges are, is okay because the numbers are written right on the tool. Besides, if you're like me, you'll usually just experiment with pulling the wire through different holes anyway until one actually works. When working with small, braided, hair-pullingly frustrating communication wires, be sure to accidentally cut the wire about 2-3 times before discovering that there is a totally different, separate wire stripper for stranded wire, because, once again, electricity hates you. Always keep the stripper perpendicular to the wire to avoid nicking it, and then try to avoid thinking of double-entendre jokes using the word "stripper" to tell your buddies later, because that is inappropriate.

If you're stripping coaxial cable, you'll first need to decide whether to join the 21st century and get a TV with HDMI cables for crying out loud. However, if you're an antique dealer, or living in your grandma's basement, or both, you may have no choice but to deal with coax cable. This type of cable requires a special stripping device that I know you don't have in your toolkit, or you wouldn't be reading this book, so I recommend either just buying a new cable, or rooting around in that box of old electrical stuff in your dad's garage next to the mag wheels he still has from his '72 Barracuda and seeing if he has one.

Project: Installing a Dimmer Switch

IF YOU GREW UP WITH A HANDYMAN DAD, you know there's more to installing a light switch than changing around a few wires. There's understanding how electricity works, how electricity doesn't work, how electricity causes a new, reality distorting feeling in an extremity previously unaccustomed to surges of high voltage, and, finally, learning new, elegantly creative curse words. Now it's your turn.

Recommended Tools:
- Hammer
- Wire cutters with those plastic grips that keep sliding off
  - Okay, you can't find your wire cutters so just use that tiny, blunted cutting area at the base of your needle nose pliers jaws
    - All right, can't find those either so... oh, wait here are the wire cutters. I forgot I was using them as a doorstop for the basement door.
  - Huh. Here is the needle nose pliers, too, wedged against the wire cutters because they kept slipping and letting the door slam.

- Okay, so now the wire cutters won't open because they got super rusty when the sump pump stopped working last April when we had the big rain and it flooded the basement.
    - So did the needle nose pliers.
    - Guess I know what I'm getting for Christmas.
- (Eyeing propane torch) I wonder what the melting temperature of 16-gauge electrical wire is...
- Wire strippers
- Screwdriver with head too large to fit in tiny wall plate screw slots
- Small promotional screwdriver in the shape of a suppository you picked up at a proctologist's convention 5 years ago when you were taking a shortcut to the parking ramp
- Hot wire checker
- Computer with Google search to find out what a "hot wire checker" is
- Oh, you meant "voltage tester"; that I've heard of
- Wish I had one (sound of car leaving to go to hardware store)

Replacing a normal on/off light switch with a new, 2-way dimmer switch in your kitchen or bathroom offers a much wider lighting palette – from bright, blinding daylight, to murky, toe-stubbing dimness. Installing one is an easy project, and by easy I mean you should only have to go back to the hardware store about once. Twice if it's raining or snowing and your wiper blades are old and streaky. Here are the steps, not necessarily in an order that will keep you from getting zapped.

1) Take off the switch's faceplate, making sure to let at least one of the tiny screws fall behind the refrigerator, where you can discover it next spring when you pull the fridge out for cleaning after failing to come up with a good enough excuse to avoid another project.
2) Oh, just for safety, you should double-check that you turned off the correct circuit break MMMmmmmMMM MMM MMMMM MMVrvvrvrvrrrMM MMMMMuh oh MMMMM UHUHUHUHU MMOWWWWW UMUMMMU MUZZUMMM okay just rideMMMM it out VRMMRRMMMRM mmmmmmmmmmmm mmmrmmm... Okay, so that was just a little buzz. Don't worry, in my experience, the feeling in your fingers will come back in about an hour or two. You now understand why Frankenstein's monster had trouble coming up with verbs and indefinite articles after his little jolt, as all you can seem to say is "wire bad." Now may also be a good time to take a break and look up some phone numbers of reputable electricians like your wife wanted you to do, just in case the feeling doesn't come back, or you're still seeing ten fingers on each hand.
3) Using your hot wire checker, test each wire and see if any of the needles move, or, if you're feeling particularly adventurous, just poke

around the box with your fingers. A hot wire checker is especially useful in convincing anyone who happens to be around you that you really know anything about what you're doing, as it has lots of knobs, wires, and probes, and occasionally beeps confidently, kind of like a tricorder from Star Trek, but a lot less useful for the average guy. For these projects, I usually use a non-contact tri-modulated voltage multi-spotter to double-check for voltage spikes, psoriasis, or scurvy in the lines. Note: you may not have to do this if your house's shots are up to date.

4) Most dimmer switches are larger than a normal on/off switch, so it's a good idea to calculate the volume of your electrical box to make sure your new switch will fit. Too many wires crammed into a box can cause dangerous overheating, short circuiting, drowsiness, dizziness, weakness, anxiety, insomnia, nausea, loss of appetite, diarrhea, constipation, dry mouth, yawning, and fires. If you are having a hard time fitting all of the wires back in the switch box, you are experiencing a common home-improvement effect called "inescapable spatial annoyance." This is the same effect that occurs when you're trying to refold a map, or roll up a sleeping bag, or re-pack a suitcase, or anything that needs to fit back into the same space it came out of, as you are convinced there is some fifth plane of existence that only tent manufacturers and Albert Einstein's ghost know how to manipulate. You can calculate the volume of an electrical box by first measuring

the depth using a bifurcated radial box caliper, then add one for each hot or neutral wire, 6.2 for a ground wire, divide by 2 for each 14-gauge wire (unless it's red), then multiply that by the circumference of the moon, find the radius of an average orange by digging up your old geometry book from high school because there was a chapter about circumferences in there somewhere, and, finally, throw these calculations in the trash, because you already bought the dimmer switch and there's no way you're making another trip back to the hardware store today.

5) Make the connections for your new dimmer by taking the ends of your wires and bending them clockwise, or, if you're in Australia, counter-clockwise. Tighten them securely under the connecting screws until they slip out and you have to start again.

6) Cross your fingers, read some tea leaves, drop a fork, hang a horseshoe on a lady bug, or whatever other superstition will make you feel better, and turn the switch to the circuit breaker back on.

If your switch is working correctly, it's time to pinch yourself in wonder that the fire department isn't currently beating your door down with an ax because of the flames. If it isn't working, consider just covering it with a decorative plaque with a quote about family on it and buy an adjustable candle.

Energy Savers

ENERGY EFFICIENCY IS A HOT TOPIC in home improvement these days, with highly paid corporate engineering gurus flying around the country in their private jets, sipping water hypothermically extracted from free-range brown rice, and being taken to biodegradable five-star hotels in stretch limos in order to invent a new water coupling for your guest bathroom faucet that can save you 3 cents every year. Scientific advances have not only given us new kinds of light bulbs that do everything but turn on within 10 seconds, they've also provided us with new and lengthy and mind-bogglingly mandatory energy regulations that you need a team of android super-lawyers to decipher. By the time this book comes out, you'll probably be being forced to bathe in reclaimed lawn dew and provide 33% of your electrical energy from a solar furnace powered by banana peels and your own skin cells. Just remember; the money you save on energy-efficient home upgrades can also help pay for all of the mistakes or injuries that occurred when you were installing them, thus completing the handyman's great circle of life and debt.

Upgrade Your Thermostat
Replacing your current, old, round, possibly coal-powered thermostat that gives you a comforting "click" when it turns on in the winter with a new,

highly efficient, brain-meltingly complex thermostat can save you up to $100 per year on your heating bill ($23,000 if you live in Canada or Buffalo). Most modern thermostats incorporate technology from something called "Skynet," which I assume is yet another new mandatory national standard. They are able to determine not only current temperatures and times of day, but also mood swings, tantrums, and marital squabbles in order to properly cool or heat occupants. Some thermostats are even controllable by a website or app on your phone, so you can really mess with your spouse or roommate when you're at the office.

Replace Light Bulbs

Replacing your current, reliable, warm and cheery incandescent light bulbs with cold, poison-mercury-filled CFL bulbs that have the illumination reaction time of a dead sloth can not only save you energy dollars, but also calories, when you decide you just don't need that box of deep-fried barbecue egg rolls from the deep freeze in your toe-stubbingly dark garage; you'll just have leftover jello tonight. CFL bulbs can last up to 10 years longer than incandescent bulbs, which makes sense, because about 8 of those years are spent just getting to seeable brightness after you turn them on. New LED bulbs are the latest development in lighting, using the same technology found in your garish, blinking Christmas lights to bring you less money in your bank account because these things are really expensive. But keep in mind they can last up to 25 years, which light bulb manufacturers apparently know because they have invented time travel and have done all of the proper light bulb expectancy experiments in the future.

Installing Low-flow Fixtures

For those of you over 50, the idea of anything "low flow" may cause you to smile uneasily and instinctively cross your legs. But what we're talking about here are plumbing items (again, not biological, uncross your legs) that can reduce your home water consumption by 30% (faucet aerators), 40% (shower heads), or even 100% (corks). Low-flow devices can also save money on your heating bill, unless you have teenagers in the house who shower about every hour, in which case it's not going to matter anyway so just forget it. But for the rest of you, by using a standard calculation to determine your current energy loss (BTUs per gallon per degree Fahrenheit x degrees temperature difference x gallons per year = BTUs per year), you will discover that you really don't remember what a BTU is, and this really looks a lot like algebra, and you got a C- in that, so just forget that, too.

Insulation

If you're not familiar with insulation, it's that stuff that rains down on you when you open the attic door and then makes you itch the rest of the day and wonder if you just got cancer. Adding insulation to your attic is not only another great way to spend money, it also has the added value of increasing the heating and cooling efficiency of your home, unless you install it in the wrong place, in which case, congratulations! You're just like the rest of us. Insulation can be blown, sprayed, foamed, extruded, batted, emulsified, embalmed, harangued, humiliated, and many other vague verbs of which you're not sure the meaning. I recommend the kind that my dad used because it had the Pink Panther on it, and we really liked those movies.

PART THREE: PLUMBING
The Liquid Male Ego Crusher

Plumbing Basics

THE TITLE OF THIS CHAPTER is meant to be a joke, as there is nothing basic about plumbing. It is the most disheartening form of home improvement and should be approached with all of the care and caution with which you would approach a rabid cougar trapped in your basement next to your leaking water heater shutoff valve. If you do feel the need to somehow "prove your manhood" or "refinance your home because of accidental catastrophic flooding," you've been duly warned. Braver men than you, some with actual degrees from Rick's Plumbing & Porcelain Fixture College, have attempted the most basic of plumbing procedures and come away crying, or maybe just wet – it's tough to tell when the water is just spraying everywhere. If you still feel the need to proceed because of some unmet manly deficiency which I don't want to know about, or a strange fascination with wet floors, then you've been warned, although probably not as much as your wife would have preferred. As Shakespeare wrote when he was knee-deep in sewage after forgetting to close the stop valve when someone backed up the toilet after Thanksgiving dinner, "The better part of Valour, is Discretion," which in today's language means, "Always have your 'Call Cooper's For Broken Poopers' phone number handy before inviting the in-laws over for Sunday dinner."

Although most major plumbing jobs, such as replacing a water heater, or replacing the water heater you broke because you tried replacing the previous water heater yourself, should be left to a professional with a name like "Chuck" driving a van with an anthropomorphic plunger painted on the side, there are some jobs you can attempt yourself. I'll give you a few of the most basic ones, which you are now probably already tuning out because you're thinking that "Anthropomorphic Plunger" is a great band name.

Project: Fixing a Leaky Faucet

UNLESS YOU'RE LIVING IN A TIME WARP in the Old West or a Greenpeace compound, you have faucets in your house. But, just like your body after high school, these eventually wear out, which you can tell when your faucet has developed symptoms more common with an older man's urology issues but which can't, unfortunately, be fixed with the bladder control medications you see during the evening news. You can probably fix a leaky kitchen faucet in about an hour, depending on how many times you have to go back to Home Depot to finally get the correct rubber washers. Here are the steps.

Recommended Tools:
- Opposable thumbs
- The wisdom of Solomon, the strength of Hercules, the stamina of Atlas, the power of Zeus, the courage of Achilles, and the speed of Mercury
- Screwdriver
- No, not that one, a Phillips screwdriver
- Adjustable wrench with stuck adjuster wheel because you left it outside when you were fixing the lawnmower
- Apparently, lots and lots of something called

"O" rings

First, you will need to determine what kind of faucet you have. There are three main kinds: A ball faucet contains a ball; a cartridge faucet contains a cartridge; a ceramic disk faucet contains a ceramic disk. Now that you have determined the gender of your faucet, you'll need to examine it to see where the leak is coming from, which, surprisingly, has nothing to do with the gender, but everything to do with what cost, kind, and frustration level of repair will be needed.

1) Turn off the water supply for both the hot and cold pipes under the sink. These usually have football-shaped handles to remind you that you could be watching the Packers playing the Vikings instead of digging through moldy towels under your sink.
2) Cover the drain of the sink with a rag, dog toy, or mildewed sponge to keep your wedding ring from falling into the garbage disposal, which, considering you are reading this book, is inevitable.
3) Now is a good time to consider hiring a professional National Geographic documentary camera crew to film you taking apart the faucet, as there are approximately 3,778 different parts in the average faucet, all of them wet and vaguely similar. You will need to keep track of which of the exact same-looking small washer you took off first, before taking off the exact same-looking smallish washer next, so that you have at least a 50/50 chance of getting

it right when you put it back together.
4) Take your old parts to your hardware store. The friendly Hardware Person there can help you locate the correct replacement for the millions of different possible parts you have brought them, even though they can see that none of them are broken.
5) Some faucets have slow water flow because of mineral deposits, which are graciously provided by your Local Water Company, along with swimming pool grade chlorine, at no extra charge. You can clean these out with a small screwdriver or penknife, depending on how many times you drop the screwdriver down the faucet pipe, or if you even know what a "penknife" is.
6) Fix your faucet.
7) After reassembling your faucet, you may see a few extra parts lying around that you didn't notice before. Don't worry; this happens to the best of us, and it may just be your wife playing a joke on you, different than the one she did when she said, "I do." Having extra parts just means that you have been incredibly efficient in your repairs, and may actually know more than the faucet manufacturer, who you now suspect may have just been trying to rip you off by putting those extra things in there in the first place.
8) If your water flow is still low, check your aerator for blockage. This is usually caused by too much cheese in the diet, and can be fixed by enjoying a long afternoon of not ever doing plumbing again.

9) Place a pan of water under the faucet so that when it starts to drip again, usually in the middle of the night, you will have ample warning to dodge the plumber's business card magnet your wife will be throwing at you.

Congratulations! You are now able to say you survived your first home improvement plumbing job without even burning the house down, even though you weren't even remotely working with fire. You're ready to tackle your next job, although you might want to check out that dripping sound coming from under the sink first.

Tip Time: Soldering Copper Pipe

IF YOU ARE AN AMBITIOUS HOME IMPROVEMENT PLUMBING GUY, or just happen to like fire, you may consider learning how to solder your own copper pipes for some of your plumbing projects. This is not as hard as it may sound, because of course just saying the words "pipe soldering" is pretty easy, but actually doing it is another matter.

Recommended Tools:
- Propane torch (Yes! Fire! Where do I get one?!)
- Lead-free, bio-dynamic, organic pasture-raised solder
- Pipe cutter
- Tinning flux (or, in a pinch, fluxing tin)
- Wet rag (Note: not a euphemism for "wife")
- Absence of incessantly spurting water

Note: as with most other projects, try to do this when your wife is away, as she may not understand why you are yelling "ouch!" from the basement so often. Here we go:

1) Always be sure to turn off the main water supply. This will be located in the dustiest and most spider-infested area of your basement,

next to a dead mouse. This might be a good time to mention that most deadly Black Widow spider bites occur during plumbing repairs.

2) You may want to keep a fire extinguisher nearby, just in case things get out of control. Come to think of it, you may just want to carry one around with you in a holster on all of your projects.

3) As with many things, such as heart surgery or making a good pizza, preparation is the key to success and an emergency-room-less day. Always make sure your joints are clean and well fluxed, if you get what I mean, which I don't think I do.

4) Your propane torch comes with a regulator and tip combination and instructions, which you will probably ignore because you want to get right to the fire part. The igniter for the torch is operated by squeezing the handle, which produces sparks, which then can ignite the gas. This is also useful for scaring the dog.

5) Cut your tubing with a pipe cutter, which is a scary instrument that looks like something they used in <u>The Godfather</u> to threaten the fingers of stoolies. Keep rotating the tool around the pipe, slowly tightening after each turn, over and over, until your wrist falls off.

6) Clean the area to be fitted with an emery cloth, which is basically just sandpaper but with a fancy college name. You must remove all burrs; otherwise your joint will leak, which, disturbingly, is what my doctor told me at my last physical.

7) Flux the joint. Again, not a euphemism; stop

laughing, this is serious; we're working with fire here.
8) Turn on your torch and try not to stare at the beautiful blue flame.
9) Solder your pipes, making sure not to do it wrong so you can't sue me. Use the wet rag to protect flammable objects such as wood joists or your fingers.
10) Resist the temptation to go outside and use the torch to light ants on fire.
11) Really, just turn off your torch.
12) Turn the water back on.
13) Pray.
14) Swear wetly.
15) Turn the water back off.
16) Repeat steps 7-13 until the project is complete.

Once you know how to properly solder a copper pipe, you'll have the necessary skills, tools, and knowledge to know you never want to do that again.

Project: Unclogging a Drain

OCCASIONALLY, WHICH IN HOME IMPROVEMENT LANGUAGE MEANS "it will inevitably happen at the most inopportune time," you will encounter a clogged sink, shower, or bathtub drain. Sometimes this is only a plugged P-trap, but I'm not going to judge you for your personal health issues, and I would also suggest not mentioning such a thing to your friends. Your best friend in these cases is usually a plunger, which probably says a lot about who you choose who to hang around with. In most cases, a little elbow grease can release the clog, although, occasionally a little knee or leg grease may be called for. However, sometimes the clog is just too stubborn, like a two year old who won't eat his lima beans, which, come to think of it, may be what's clogging your sink. In any case, here are some tips that may help you out of your jam without the use of convenient and helpful chemicals.

Recommended Tools:
- Hammer, maybe a really big one. Maybe even a sledge hammer, or a big rock tied to a stick
- Allen wrench (or "Allan" wrench if you're British)
- Bucket
- Ice for bucket
- Cold beverage to put in ice in bucket

- Pipe wrench (the thing that looks like a guy with his mouth stuck open in fear because he's doing plumbing)
- Rags. Lots and lots of rags
- Slip joint pliers (Note: this is not street slang for drugs)
- I don't think you got enough rags. Get some more.
- Shop vacuum (maybe two or three, depending on how good you are at this)

<u>Optional tools:</u>
Female person who is angrily looking up replacement costs of engagement rings while glaring at you sideways wondering if she believes that you really just accidentally knocked her ring into the sink.

1) First, if your clog is in a deep-set floor backpipe with a C-ball drain-trap, remove the back flow preventer with a cold (NOT HOT) chisel, keeping the retaining ring clockwise to the auger nut. (Translation: Call a plumber.)
2) Usually, the clog is caused by a gunky wad of hair, which would NOT make a good band name. You can retrieve this out of the drain by making a small hook out of a paper clip, or using a Professional Barbed Poky Plastic Stick such as I keep under the sink cabinet for just such an occasion. Remove the drain stopper, then poke the stick into the drain, making sure to get it stuck on some unseen drain part that refuses to let go, so that you wonder if there's some kind of Drain Troll down there who lives off of gunky hair and who's grabbing your Poky

Stick as penance for trying to douse him with Drano earlier. Keep at it until you pull out a wad of hair, which you can then show your female house dwellers, who will then pronounce it "gross," even though they're most likely the ones who made it.

3) If your clog is in a sink, it may be in the drain trap under the sink, which is the U-shaped pipe you always thought should just go straight down so it doesn't get clogged. You can usually easily remove this for cleaning or ring rescuing, but considering the usual luck of most homeowners, expect something to go wrong.

4) If your clog is particularly tough and immune to Professional Barbed Poky Plastic Sticks, you may need to employ the use of a snake, and not some rare, hair-gunk eating reptile from Papua New Guinea you can rent from the pet store, which would be extremely cool. No, this snake is a long, flexible steel rope that you can attach to your cordless drill and use to perform a violent colonoscopy on your toilet. A 15- to 20-foot 1/4" snake should be sufficient for most homes, or you can try a 1/4" 20- to 15-foot snake if that doesn't work. If you're unclogging a sink, you'll have to remove the P-trap first (see introductory paragraph), but if you are unclogging a toilet, I'm so sorry.

5) After attaching the snake to your drill, shove the snake into the toilet while twisting it and turning the drill, making sure to splash as much toilet water on your face and arms as possible. Eventually, you will reach the clog, which I don't like thinking about, but since it's

your toilet, it doesn't bother me quite as much. Reverse the drill and begin pulling the snake back out of the drain, all the while trying not to think about where it's been, and what lives there, and why you even think that something could live there, and if you're going to get syphilis from the splashing toilet water, until the end of the snake snaps out of the drain, possibly with some horror attached to it they wouldn't even show in a Quentin Tarantino movie. Now you can coil the snake up in a bucket and stick it in the garage someplace and wonder why you ever thought about doing this in the first place, on account of your chronic P-trap issues.

Now that your drain is finally unclogged, consider getting everyone in your family crew cuts to help prevent further blockages, and good luck sleeping tonight as you dream about rabid P-traps and New Guinean toilet snakes.

Project: Replacing a Toilet

FOR THIS NEXT JOB, it will help to remember that there was a time, back when mankind was young and the stars hung bright and clean in the new heavens, and the air was crisp and pure, the rain was sweet, and we ate fresh fruits and nuts, and occasionally a raw rabbit, and then more fresh fruits, that we had to poop in the woods. So be grateful that, even though you are about to perform the equivalent of a residential bowel resection, at least you get to do it indoors out of the rain.

While most of us will choose a fully licensed, germ-laden, possibly plague-ridden toilet plumber for replacing a toilet, you might be one of those guys who like new adventures, or acquiring new tools, skills, or diseases. Or maybe you just lost a bet with your brother-in-law. Here are some suggestions that can help you replace your offending porcelain excretion portal with a minimal amount of germ contact and keep you out of the dysentery ward at your local hospital.

Recommended Tools:
- Wax toilet ring
- Brass toilet bolts
- Three French hens
- Two turtledoves

- 14 pairs of concentric rubber gloves
- Inability to sense 12 years of almost palpable toilet germs which you just know are invading your skin through 14 pairs of rubber gloves
- Toilet crane
- In lieu of toilet crane, large man named Lars or Sven who isn't afraid of death by frenzied toilet germs
- World's largest heavy-duty sealable baggie designed specifically for used toilet disposal
- Petition to Congress asking why no manufacturers are forced to produce large, heavy-duty sealable toilet baggies
- Mental note to use Sealable Toilet Baggies for new neo-punk metal band name

    I'm not going to ask you why you want to replace your toilet. For most people, that's a private matter, like asking whom they voted for in the last presidential election or why they married a musician. If you've already shopped for and bought a new toilet, you have now used the word "waste" more often than you will the rest of your entire life. Note: be sure your new toilet matches the standard 12" distance from the waste pipe to the wall, or your toilet installation will produce results similar to when your uncle Ben complained about all of the cheese he ate watching the game last night, and now you have two inches of standing water in the hallway outside your bathroom. Also, if your toilet is located next to a door, measure to make sure your new toilet does not extend farther forward than your old one, or you will be in danger of being featured in the next issue of <u>Home Handyman's</u> "Great Gaffes and Bountiful Blunders" with an unflattering cartoon. Now on to (and I'm so glad I get to use this phrase at least once in my life) "pulling a toilet."

1) First, shut the water to the toilet off, or you can cancel next summer's trip to Yellowstone, as you will already have experienced Old Faithful in your bathroom, plus your finances will be drained because of a large bill from Todd's Suck & Dry. Disconnect the supply line from the back of the tank.
2) Flush the toilet until all of the water from the tank is gone, and the Tidy Bowl Man is struggling to scramble up the sides of the tank using a tiny rope ladder.
3) Put on your 14 pairs of concentric rubber gloves, and, using a sponge or shop vac, get someone else to sop up the rest of the water out of the toilet bowl. Dispose of this water in an appropriate place, such as the La Brea Tar Pits, or an active volcano.
4) Remove the metal toilet bolts securing your current toilet to the floor. These will be frozen tight from years of leaky toilet action, so make sure you strip the heads off of them with your cheap socket set you got free with a Jiffy Lube oil change last year.
5) Use a hacksaw blade to cut the frozen bolt just under the nut head, which is precisely what you are already calling yourself for attempting this project. Note: get more knuckle-maiming tips for frozen bolts and screws in Chapter 27: Freeing Stuck Nuts, Bolts and Screws.
6) Try not to think about what the toilet has been

used for the past 10 to 20 years.

7) Try not to think about the time you had stomach flu and diarrhea for two days straight last year and utilized this toilet to its full capacity.

8) Try not to think about when you had your colonoscopy and had to drink that nasty liquid that cleans you out and you practically lived in this bathroom and spent so much time with this toilet you named it "Tex."

9) Try not to remember that obscure report you read about years ago then completely forgot about until it just now popped into your head that said there are about 12 billion germs around the base of the average toilet.

10) Grasping the toilet as if it were a 28-pound diseased, malignant white porcelain virus, lift the toilet straight up, making sure to let it slip and drop at least once onto your foot.

11) Resist the urge to peer down the opening of the waste receptacle, as you will go blind like Spock did in that episode of <u>Star Trek</u> where he looked at the flashing lights inside the box that was supposed to be an incredibly ugly alien.

12) Install the new wax toilet ring and brass toilet bolts onto the edge of the um… the uh… waste receptacle. Excuse, me; I need to get some air.

13) Lift your new, doomed toilet onto the bolts and wax, sealing the waste receptacle shut as if it were the Fifth Door to Hades. Tighten the bolts, making sure to let the adjustable wrench you're using slip and scar the side of your new toilet before it's even been used.

14) Reconnect the supply line, turn the water back

on, let the tank fill, check for leaks, take one yourself, and flush.
15) Vow never, ever to so something this disgusting again.

Even though this is probably the most revolting job you'll ever perform, it makes for great bragging rights to the guys at the office, who will be impressed that you did something so nasty yet cool, and that you're not retching from a terminal case of toilet gingivitis. Now, go see your wife, who is asking you to plunge the guest bathroom toilet because it's backed up again.

PART FOUR: INDOOR PROJECTS

Where it's Easier to Reach the Phone to Call for Help

Project: Build a Saw Horse

SAWHORSES ARE ANOTHER ONE OF THOSE GREAT home-improvement accessories that are not only practical, but they make people think you know what you're doing just by seeing them stacked in your garage. This handy helper is great for raising projects off the floor, to make space so you can shove other unfinished projects under it. They're easy to make if you know how, but if you don't, well, you should probably just buy some.

Recommended Tools:
- Hammer
- Horse sawn in half
- What? Okay, so apparently there's no real horse involved here; my bad, sorry
- Some wood, preferably not still in log format
- A saw: this can be a table saw, hand saw, chop saw, circular saw, square saw, chain saw, see saw, or one of those guys who can just break wood with his bare hands
- 2x4s you salvaged from last year's aborted picnic table project
- Cordless drill
- Screws (or, if you're in a real hurry, duct tape)

1) Cut the 2x4s into four legs of a comfortable working height. If you're short on wood (or just

cheap), you can try using just three legs, but you're setting yourself up for some awfully frustrating projects. I recommend building your horse a little taller than you think you'll need; if it's too tall, you can always cut the legs down later and get that extra uneven wobble effect to boot.

2) Cut a bevel on one edge of each of the legs. I recommend an angle of about 55 degrees counter to the square line, or 28 degrees from the board edge, but no more than 33 degrees offset from the inclination biscuit, until Jupiter is aligned with Mars.

3) Cut the cross piece, or back of the horse, from the remaining wood, which at this point is a piece about 18 inches long, because you used most of it up on your tall legs.

4) With the beveled edge of each leg set flush against the cross piece, drill three pilot holes through each leg, into the cross piece, and out the other side into your concrete floor, snapping off the tip of your drill bit. Do this four times.

5) Using screws screwed through the pilot holes you made for each leg, assemble your World's Narrowest Sawhorse. Notice how your screws are too short and barely reach the cross piece. Go to the hardware store for longer screws.

6) Screw your new, longer screws through the pilot holes you made for each leg. Notice how your screws are now too long and are poking through the top of the cross piece. Instead of going to the store again:
   a) Grind the points of the screws down

with the rotary grinding tool you asked for for Christmas two years ago but have never used.
b) Recharge your thoroughly dead rotary grinding tool because it's been sitting new in the box for two years.
c) Smash the screws down with your hammer.
7) Once all of your legs are assembled, stand your sawhorse up like a trembling, newborn calf. Measure down from the cross piece about 8 inches, and with a scrap piece of wood you just found from your abandoned deck planter project, create four spreader braces roughly 28 degrees lateral to 115 top and 65 posterior bottom for a total of 180 degrees, or 25 from square, depending on if the moon is in the Seventh house.
8) Screw the spreader braces into place using either your too-short or too-long screws.

You should now have a fully functional and battle-ready saw horse, suitable for tearing apart for scrap wood for your next project, which I think might be that picnic table again.

Project: Painting a Room

IT IS A WELL-KNOWN FACT that nothing adds value and freshness to old, stale decor than the new carpet you have to buy after you spill paint on the old carpet when you try to add value and freshness to your old stale decor by repainting a room. So, while you angrily bask in that new carpet smell, let's revisit some valuable tips you should have learned before your room-remodeling budget ballooned.

Recommended Tools:
- Hammer (for opening paint cans when you can't find that thing you usually use as a bottle opener)
- Old, stiff, no-knap paint roller you saved from your last job but couldn't quite get all of the paint out of
- Cheap dollar store brush that sheds bristles like a dog with the mange
- Lots of drop cloths, consisting mostly of old towels, the drapes from your last house, and pieces of cardboard from the packaging your unused exercise bike came in.

The first step in updating any room with a fresh, new paint color is deciding what your sex and marital status is. If you are a married male, be advised that no matter what color decision you make, it will most likely be wrong, as the Tasteful Color Sensor organ in most males is hidden behind the I Just Want To Get This Done Because the Cubs Come On At Three organ. According to the Internet, which never lies, **paint color is one of the greatest sources of DIY disagreements for couples**. So, if you are wise, you will let your wife decide whether "Pale Pre-Cambrian Aruba Sunset Allure" or "Post-War Parisian Festooned Mango Melt" will be the color you have to stare at in the bathroom for the next 5 years while you try to read your <u>Sports Illustrated</u>. If you are a single male, go back to watching that rerun of <u>The Rat Patrol</u> you've seen 6 times already; what are you doing here? If you are a female: yes, dear.

But before you can choose a color, you will need a requisite visit to your local Home Improvement Asylum, where miles of color swatches await you, conveniently arrayed in helpful rainbow rows, from dull, dusty dirt colors to super-fashionable-retina-burning hues. Most home decor magazines, afraid of being "boring" and "gauche" and "not selling magazines," will challenge you to make a "bold" statement by choosing "aggressive" color palettes you'll have to "repaint" in two years because your neighbor who you thought was your "friend" made an offhand yet still somehow catty comment about how "Vermillion Tahiti Salsa" was no longer the best red to choose for dining nooks and recommends "Crushed Twilight Plum Nubbins," which was the color Angelina Jolie used in her $100,000 kitchen remodel your neighbor saw on <u>Good Morning America</u> last Tuesday when you were probably sleeping in. So be prepared for a weekend painting a color you will most likely need to apply while wearing sunglasses. The alternative route suggests a more soothing palette of subtle grays or tans, which, while decidedly boring, will complement any decor, and will be much easier to apply, because it is the color you already have on your walls.

1) As any professional painter knows, preparation is the key to success, but, since you are most likely not a professional painter, you should prepare for something less. Here's how:
2) Remove all outlet plates, making sure you accidentally touch the live, exposed plug to remind you again that electricity, while yet invisible, can still make you curse.
3) Use only name-brand, expensive, hard-to-find green masking tape specially designed for taping off areas you don't want paint to get on, such as door trim or the dog. Do not be tempted to use that old roll of dried up masking tape you found in a box of 1970s woodworking magazines from your dad, even if it is free. You may use duct tape if you enjoy extending weekend projects into repeated visits to emergency psych wards.
4) Completely remove all of the sticky gunk your daughter used for her Donny Osmond/Backstreet Boys/**One Direction or whatever is the current boy band** posters from the walls, while making sure to conveniently lose those posters in next Monday's trash pickup.
5) Fill the door knob hole in the wall left when your son opened it in anger when you took away his <u>Zombie Bikini Apocalypse 4</u> game

because he drew mustaches on his sister's One Direction posters, even though they are pretty annoying (the posters, not the children). Use as many tubes of caulk as necessary.
6) "Lap marks" are not the incriminating results of a poor choice of a weekend activity with the guys but are caused by rolling wet paint on an area of paint that is too dry. To avoid these, only paint walls that are 18 inches wide.
7) Paint the room in this order: trim, ceiling, dog, carpet, angry wife, your best pants, antique dresser you forgot to cover, dog again, and walls.
8) Use cotton drop cloths, not plastic. This way, you can see reminders of your past mistakes the next time you paint.

And, as with any home-improvement project, always leave room to pause and enjoy the results of your hard work and dedication. So take a break, step back, and realize you just put your foot in the paint tray.

Project: Wallpapering a Room

ANYONE CAN PAINT A ROOM (see previous chapter), or a room and a carpet, or a room, carpet, and dog, but it takes a special skill to enhance your decor with that unique, insoluble glue that only wallpaper can bring to your rug. Adding wallpaper is an easy way to add spice to a space, or, as I prefer to say, an easy way to an involuntary mental evaluation. You can take a room from dull to dashing, with a brief stop at Xanax, in a matter of hours, or even minutes, if you own a staple gun. Although it may seem intimidating, like performing brain surgery with a butter knife and gluey, sticky fingers, these simple tips can help anyone master the art of wallpaper hanging without having your house end up on a ventilator for the rest of its life.

Recommended Tools:
- Hammer
- Taping Knife
- Xanax
- Wallpaper
- Water

First, you must choose your pattern. We prefer a solid, flat, white pattern, which, albeit boring, makes it a whole lot easier to match the seams. You, or more accurately, your spouse, will prefer a more whimsical or cozy pattern, such as can be found at your local Home Improvement Giant Metal Cavern. Patterns for living rooms will have elegant names, such as "Prussian Quilt (Act Two: Under the Chestnut Tree) Damask," or "Oxfordshire Penmanship Improved Harvard Law School Crosshatch." Bathroom patterns generally include stripes, as these are the hardest seams to match and Wallpaper Manufacturers are cruel jerks. Wallpaper designed for kitchens will have more practical names, such as "Chocolate Pudding Toddler Splatter," "How Did The Dog Accident Get That High?!" or "Traditional Tuesday Night Spaghetti and Meatballs Rug Trip."

As with most home-improvement projects, such as arson for insurance purposes, preparation is the key to success. Make sure you always wallpaper in one direction, left or right, in order to keep your pattern consistent. If you have already started papering up and down, congratulations! Your involuntary mental evaluation is just around the corner. However, no matter how good your technique, the end pieces will never match, because your house still holds a grudge from last year's botched paint job. For this reason, you should start papering from behind a door, so that anyone entering the room to tell you that you're cursing too loud and the children can hear you can knock you off your ladder, and also so that the mismatched last pattern will end up above the door, where it can cover the hole left by the smoke alarm you tried to install last year.

1) First, cut sheets four inches longer than the balustrade, or cornice hens, but not less than three inches from the inseam while recumbent to the cosine except during daylight saving time or three hours before swimming, unless you are using the metric system, which means you need to convert to megajoules and move to Canada.
2) Next, using a paint roller, consider that this is your last chance to just paint the room and save yourself a lot of grief. Using a barely damp sponge, mop your brow; this is the last time you will feel good today.
3) Then, using a 6-inch taping knife, whatever that is, carefully wallpaper your room.

After a few hours of wallpapering, you may experience a disturbing sense of disorientation, as if you were living in an M. C. Escher sketch, where patterns fold in on patterns, and seams dare you, laughing, to match them as they dance away. Now is not the time for panic; that can wait until your wife gets home. Now is the time to step back, probably pulling some wallpaper with you, and find the note with the phone number on it for the Professional Wallpaper Hanger your spouse wanted you to call. It will be stuck to the bottom of your shoe.

Whichever way you choose to paper your home, whether by using a professional wallpaper hanger or a professional therapist, you can rest assured that you have added value and style to your home, which will last at least until you realize simultaneously that the cat is missing and there's a strange lump in the wall.

Tip Time: Wall Anchors: The Hardware Industry's Way of Giving You An In-Home Mental Health Assessment

AT SOME POINT IN YOUR DUBIOUS HOME-IMPROVEMENT CAREER, you'll need to hang a heavier object than your favorite "chimp with a boom box" poster left over from college, such as a mirror, shelf, or newly framed "chimp with a boom box" poster, at which your wife is already shaking her head in disapproval. This means you'll need to pound a nail or drill a screw into something more substantial than just your drywall, or, if you live in an older house with plaster walls, you might as well start getting ready to clean up the broken wall chunks now.

How to Find a Stud
Just look in the mirror! Ha ha! Now that we have that obligatory joke out of the way, let's get serious about stud finding. Single ladies, you may want to highlight this part, just in case.

Finding wall studs is a common task in home improvement, as, just like politicians, you are either going to want to pound something into one, or avoid it all together. The easiest way to find a stud is by using an electronic stud finder, which, when drawn across a wall, will give a piercing beep whenever it encounters a stud, wire, pipe, your daughter's calcified dead hamster you told her went to heaven, or anything else remotely solid. You can pick one up at your local Home Improvement Barn by looking for an item which will be called something like "Zorcan Intelli-Sensor™ Dub-Step© Frame-Lok® with Anti-Hamster-Fail©" – pretty much any name except "stud finder." However, in some situations you won't have access to an electronic stud finder, either because the batteries in it are dead and you're out of AAs because you used the last one to power the controllers at your son's all night Wii party, or because you just don't want to go to the basement to get it. Here, then, are some other ways to locate a stud without having to use inexpensive, timesaving, and accurate electronic devices, but which will make you feel a little more like a super-resourceful guy.

1) Try removing a cover plate from an electrical outlet, and then look for the "spacing knobs" which indicate to which side of the wall the box is attached. After replacing the outlet cover, go to your computer and Google "spacing knobs" to see what exactly you are looking for. The knobs will be located next to the stud, from which you can more or less (I usually go with less) accurately determine where to pound your nail, screw your screw, or whatever it is you're trying to do to ruin your wall.
2) If your walls are drywall, use an angled flashlight and look for nail or screw indentions,

tape marks, or other blemishes that can determine where studs may be located. Frown as you wonder what inebriated bozo built this pathetic wall, just as you realize it was your father-in-law who did it for free because you were too cheap to hire a contractor.

3) Examine your baseboard or other wall trim to see where the finish nails have been affixed, which should be where the stud is located. They may be difficult to spot, unless you installed the trim yourself, in which case they are probably still waiting to be filled with putty and should be easy to locate.

4) Locate your heating and cooling duct grates, remove the plate, and see where the studs are located. Spend the rest of the day annoying your wife and children by trying to say "duct grates" as fast as possible over and over.

Wall Anchors
You won't get far down the dusty road of home improvement before hearing the wailing siren of needing to hang something on your walls and being stopped by the wall anchor police after this metaphorically incomprehensible introduction. Fortunately, the hardware community, in an ever-increasing desire to sell millions of tons of spackle, has provided a myriad of methods for you to put progressively irrelevant holes in your walls. Here are a few of the most common methods.

Expansion Anchors (The Plastic Bullet Of Security)
These are the most common forms of drywall anchors,

as proven by the fact that manufacturers include them in just about every piece of home-improvement packaging, partially as a way of saying "See! You can do this!" but mostly as a way to keep Chinese plastic factories in business. You'll need your drill and appropriately sized drill bit for these (don't be tempted to cut corners by just punching a Bic pen through the wall) and a small hammer, like the cute, tiny one your wife got in the pink Lady Fix-It tool kit her dad gave her way before you were married.

Threaded Drywall Anchors (The Reason You Bought That Dust Buster)
These beauties are one of the fastest ways to provide a secure mount for that hideous wall knick-knack your Green Bay Packer fan aunt-in-law gave you of the two cherubs kissing over the crumpled body of Fran Tarkenton so that it can be easily removed when she leaves after Christmas. However, they are a little unnerving, as when screwing them in, they leave enough drywall dust on your floor to fill a major league pitcher's chalk bag. There is also little room for mistakes, as they leave a large hole, so make sure you've read the scary chapter on drywall repair before proceeding.

Toggle Bolt Anchors (The T-shaped Brain Teaser)
Use these when you either only have the 1-inch drill bit left in your bit case because your 2-year-old nephew dropped the rest of them down your heat vent when he found your toolbox, or when you really like a mental challenge, like that puzzle made out of two bent nails your uncle gave you when you were a kid to

shut you up while he was watching golf. These can be tricky, so I've provided some helpful steps using numbers with parentheses by them.

1) Drill a hole much larger than you think should really be necessary for the size of the anchor but which the instructions say you should do.
2) Thread the shaft of the bolt onto the springy thing, making sure to let it spring out of your hand once or twice and get lost in your shag carpet, or, if you're really lucky, escape down into the heat vent into which your nephew dropped your drill bits.
3) Push the springy thing into your new, gigantic hole, making sure, on your first try, to push it too far and drop it inside the wall.
4) Either:
    a) Drive to the hardware store while coming up with some new, colorful adjectives to describe the probable inbred lineage of the inventor of the T-shaped Brain Teaser.
    b) Forget this — there's an episode of <u>Coach</u> on the oldies station I don't think I've seen yet.
5) Turn the head of the screw until the anchor tightens and secures the bolt to the wall, which will never happen in your lifetime, because the anchor is just twisting behind the wall.
6) Pull the bolt toward you until the anchor catches, then try to turn the screw at the same time to tighten the anchor, all the while humming the theme to <u>Mission Impossible</u> through clenched teeth.

7) Once the bolt is tight against the wall, realize you should have first threaded the bolt through the thing you were trying to hang on the wall, and will have to start over.
8) Repeat from step 4 until your brain explodes.

Project: Installing a New Towel Bar

IF YOU HAVE TEENAGERS IN YOUR HOUSE, you also have musty towels, because the towel hanging gene has been somehow secretly un-engineered by our public schools for the past 40 years. One possible solution to this is to install more towel hangers, in hopes that having a bunch of them around will increase the odds of your teenager being distracted from their phone long enough to think the towel hangers are actually the floor.

<u>Recommended Tools:</u>
- Hammer
- Screwdriver (no, not the drink)
- Allen wrench that came with the towel bar packaging
- New Allen wrench set from the hardware store because you accidentally dropped the Allen wrench that came with the towel bar packaging into the toilet, and you are considering it lost forever to the toilet gods, because this toilet was not flushed, and you don't care if it backs up because of it or anything, you're not going after it
- New Allen wrench set from the hardware store (metric)

- Cordless drill
- Your dad's old level – the one with three bubbles in it

It's best to try to match your new towel bar to the current decor of your bathroom, and by "best" I mean "impossible," as your current decor uses bathroom fixture models that went out of stock around the time Reagan got shot. You'll have to scour the internet for something similar, most likely with three ridges at the base instead of two, and two concentric circles on the knob instead of three, and just not quite the actual off-gold dull-brassy finish you currently have, but just close enough to distract you every time you see it. In this way, you will have a helpful, constant reminder that life is imperfect, even when, or maybe especially when, you're in the bathroom. If you've ordered your towel bar online, it is always imperative to check that is has all of the parts once it arrives, as it came all the way from China and may have lost a few things on the trip. For example, you may have received two left holders and a bent bar, which is great if you're remodeling Salvador Dali's bathroom, but physically impossible to make work in our current universe.

Once you are sure that you have all of the correct parts, or at least close enough to try to just make a go of it and see what happens, you can begin the installation process. In order to have a successful experience, be sure to follow the manufacturer's instructions carefully, which will go something like this:

TO THE INSTRUCTIONS:
With gratitude you using my firm product, from the area of my heart! Please take this manul to use in order to proceed in exactitude.

ATTENTION!
Please at the time of unrapping, to locate all assemblies with awareness for the future times. To counsl with the builder, return all assemblies without fail, so as not to corrupt reality.
Please do not use it besides the use of it, such for hands, grabers, and slippers stopping.

1) Resist the packaging for getting the assemblies in order.
2) Prepare lactation of wall studs by eqipments, then marc lactation with penceels.
3) Mesure 2,343mm to lactation of secun space. Marc lactation with penceels.
4) Produce holes.
5) Accord and pursue to point assemblies of "B" to holes, firstly with frog up, next for the poot.
6) Hit hard at the end of the bar in the form of an arc, the presure in the spring will flog the mandible.
7) Now will your bar center and proud to be the poot!

If you follow theses instructions to the letter, you will have ample evidence to show the helpful receptionists when you apply for voluntary submission to your local psych ward. To be fair, I'm sure my Chinese instructions on how to drill a simple hole in the wall would be even less intelligible to some poor soul in Beijing trying to install his mandatory Helpful Citizen Comrade Compliance-Enhancer Monitoring Camera in his breakfast nook. For our current project, though, here are some instructions in English that should help not bring down the value of your home too much.

1) Locate the best possible position for your new towel bar. This will ideally be conveniently located near a bath or shower, but could also be ingeniously placed directly above the wall charger for your teenager's cell phone.
2) Your towel bar needs to be firmly anchored into the wall so that when someone inevitably grabs it for support because they slipped on the mat that was wet from where you just gave the dog a bath and you didn't have time to clean it up because you didn't have anywhere to hang the towels which is why you are doing this project in the first place, it will cause the minimum amount of damage. The ideal way to anchor the bar would be to secure it directly to the wall studs, which occur every 16 inches, but since the Towel Bar Manufacturing Industry (Official Motto: "Pleading With Uncaring Teenagers For Over 40 Years") has apparently decided that that would be too convenient, your bars will come in choices of any length other than in increments of 16 inches. This means you will need to install...
3) Wall anchors. You can find out more about wall anchor types in the helpful chapter on "Wall Anchors: The Hardware Industry's Way of Giving You An In-Home Mental Health

Assessment." For now, let's assume you are stuck with the wimpy blue anchors that came with your towel bar packaging. First, if possible, I recommend you anchor at least one end of your bar to a wall stud, because the extra strength it provides will give you a few fewer milliseconds of stomach-dropping fear after you grab it because you slipped on the mat that was wet from where you just gave the dog a bath, etc.

4) Using the handy pictorial instructions that came with your towel bar that are written in what looks like Sanskrit with diagrams made by a highly-caffeinated ancient Egyptian who is missing a thumb, determine that you're just going to roughly guess where you should mark the holes and hope for the best.

5) Use your level to align the hole positions so that your bar will be straight and your towels won't all huddle to one side of the bar in fear.

6) Drill the holes to insert your wall anchors, which will be either one size too large or too small because you lost the correct-sized drill bits long ago.

7) Pound a wall anchor into one of your incorrectly sized holes with a hammer until it is mashed and mangled. Remove it and keep trying until one stays in or you run out of wall anchors.

8) Attach the towel bar mounting plates to your wall anchors using the screws that came with the packaging that are too big to fit in the provided wall anchors.

9) Go to the basement and spend 25 minutes

fishing through the old rusty coffee can of random screws your grandfather gave you because he already had eight more just like it and wouldn't miss it.
10) Get distracted by a cool marble you found in the coffee can and wonder if it's worth anything on eBay.
11) Using the few mismatched screws that you found that sort of go into the wall anchors, attach your towel bar mounting plates.
12) Find the tiny, almost microscopic set screw on the side of one of the towel bar posts, and, using your smallest screwdriver, scratch the side of the post about six times and gouge the wall two times before you finally are able to tighten it.
13) Attach the other post in the same fashion, until you realize you forgot to put the bar between the posts first.
14) Do that.

You are now the proud owner of a new (although slightly scratched) towel bar, ready to be ignored by every teenager in the house, who will continue to mindlessly drop their towels wherever they like, except on the wet dog.

Project: Hanging the Perfect Picture

ADDING BEAUTY AND ATTRACTIVENESS to your home or apartment with new artwork is easy when you know how. Unfortunately, I only know the hard way to do it. First, you will need something to hang on your wall. If you don't already own a picture, you are probably a guy, in which case I suggest obtaining <u>Dogs Playing Poker</u> or <u>Albert Einstein Sticking His Tongue Out</u>. If you are married, the picture has already been sitting in the den for three weeks waiting for you to put it up, so get to it already.

<u>Recommended Tools:</u>
- Hammer
- Wall anchors (See Chapter 17)
- Laser level you wanted for Christmas but never got because no one in your family knows what a laser level is
- Brittle, dried-out masking tape from your junk drawer
- Large Hadron Collider (optional)

Choosing the best place to hang the picture is your first challenge, unless this picture-hanging project was precipitated by an "Accidentally Put A Hole In The Wall With The End Of The Ladder While Trying

To Put Up A Different Picture" project, in which case you know exactly where to hang it. Having a helper, such as a wife, will aid you immensely, as they will be well practiced in telling you exactly where to go. Let's get to it.

1) Most experts recommend hanging the picture about 60 inches from the floor, but since most experts usually have a tape measurer handy, you'll probably just have to guess. Just figure that 60 inches is about as tall as that torn place on the wall where someone tried to remove one of those totally irremovable Removable Plastic Sticky Picture Hangers (As Probably Seen On TV). Mark this spot with a pencil or piece of masking tape, making sure to spend at least 5 minutes rummaging in your junk drawer to find either one of them.

2) If you are hanging a group of pictures, congratulations! Your work frustrations are about to grow exponentially. Now may be a good time to retake that physics class you bombed in high school. Using a laser level for this type of project is a great idea, because it comes with these cool glasses that make you look like Cyclops from the X-Men. Use the laser level to make a horizontal line (or vertical, if you live below the equator), which you can use to align the tops of all your pictures. The most fool-proof method for arranging your pictures is to make paper cutouts of them and arrange them using low-adhesive masking tape, but who really has time for that?

3) Once you have chosen the position for your

new picture, it might be time for a break, because when you were looking for your low-adhesive tape, which you didn't have anyway, you noticed your junk drawer was really messy, and had all kinds of bent paper clips, old coupons, and dried-out bank pens cluttering everything up, and you were about to straighten it out when you found one of those old games where you try to roll the BBs into the holes on the clown's face, and you spent 20 minutes trying to get the hard one that goes into his hat before you realized you totally forgot what you were originally doing. (Hint: You were hanging a picture.)

4) Now comes the part where you actually have to pound something into the wall. If your picture has just one hook holder on the back, breathe a sigh of relief, because you are now 50% less likely to screw this up.

5) Pound a picture hanger holder into one of the spots you already marked. (I'm assuming you have drywall walls; if you have plaster walls, your house is Old and may be worth a lot of money. Consider selling it.)

6) Make sure you use the only hammer you could find, the one with the huge head on it you keep in the garage, so that you can smash at least one of your fingers while pounding in the hanger.

7) If your picture has two hooks on the back, you are in for a treat of perpetual OCD-inducing exasperation, as it is physically impossible for someone short of Stephen Hawking to place two picture holders perfectly level with each

other. You'll need a measuring tape, a level, a calculator with cosine function, and the Large Hadron Collider in Switzerland in order to calculate exactly where to place everything.
8) Proceed to hang your picture.
9) Take extra precautions when hanging something heavy, such as a mirror, because it can cause depression and anxiety when you walk past it every day and realize you really need to get back on the treadmill. And it's crooked.

Now you can step back and enjoy your new picture with a mixed sense of accomplishment and unease, as you're still not sure if that <u>Dogs Playing Poker With Einstein</u> painting is the best choice for the guest bathroom.

Tip Time: Pulling nails

MOST OF US HAVE HAD TO PULL A NAIL at one time; it's quite possibly the first home-improvement project activity you can remember, when you were small and you were helping your grandfather salvage some boards from an old project for a new, hopefully less-mangled one. You've probably found that some nails are easier to pull than others; the rusty one that just punctured your foot because you forgot to pull it from that board from the abandoned picnic table project you left outside all winter is pretty quick to come out, but for more stubborn ones, I'll try to show you some tricks that hopefully won't require a stinging application of Bactine with a tetanus shot chaser.

First, try using a small scrap piece of wood for leverage. If you can't find a scrap piece of wood, which you almost never can, try using your screwdriver, a muddy stick from the yard, a muddy rock from the yard, a broom handle, or a dog bone, before cleverly settling on the shaft of your hammer, until you realize you need the hammer to pull the nail. Placing your leverage block next to the nail, proceed to pull up on the head of the nail until it inevitably strips off, which leads us immediately to the next paragraph.

If the nail head has been stripped or has popped off, or if you are trying to remove a stubborn finish nail that, although an inanimate object, you are sure is somehow psychologically taunting you, try this trick. Find your vise grip (it's probably still outside attached to the your snow blower where you were using it to keep the cotter pin in place so your wheel wouldn't fall off). Show the now rusty tool to your neighbor Dave, who doesn't own a snow blower, so you know his vice grip is probably still functional, and ask if you can borrow his. Using Dave's vice grip, tightly grip the nail at the base, making sure to loosen and unloosen it about 8 times before it is tight enough. Then use your claw hammer to lift the nail, using the vice grip as a brace, until the nail comes free suddenly and the hammer and vice grip fly up and knock your hat off, narrowly missing your right eye. After furtively checking to make sure that your wife didn't just see that, throw the removed nail into the nearest trash can, making sure to not notice you barely missed the can and the nail has rolled under your tire to await your next, hitherto unforeseen project.

If the nail refuses to move, or if you're just plain angry, try using a reciprocating saw to cut through the nail. This has the added advantage of using a loud power tool with teeth that not only scares the dog but has your wife subconsciously reaching for the phone to dial the ER number she has long-since memorized. As with almost all home-improvement techniques, this method has the distinct possibility of adding a new project to your list, such as the "New, Decorative Slice in the Bathroom Wall" project, the "Where Did The WiFi Go AGAIN, Dad?" project, and the "Honey... Why Is There Water Spraying Out Of The Electrical Socket?" project.

Project: Fixing Squeaks

NOTHING IS MORE ANNOYING than a squeaking [fill in the blank], except maybe getting a political robocall while the [fill in the blank] is squeaking. Note: these tips not only work for creaks and small squeals, but also for screeches, scrapes, or crepitation. If you are hearing moans, groans, wails, or lamentations, you should consult that short lady in <u>Poltergeist</u> who really knows how to clean houses.

<u>Recommended Tools:</u>
- Hammer
- Anti-squeak stuff your dad always used
- Anti-squeak stuff your father-in-law says to use
- Anti-squeak stuff you read about in the <u>Hopeless Handyman</u> magazine article that is much better informed than this book
- No mice

Squeaking Doors
If you are an average, thriving, well-adjusted member of society, you may have already discovered the advantages that doors have to offer. They keep out the cold and heat, provide security, and are an excellent way to show how angry you are by slamming them. They also, just like your knees after that ill-advised pickup basketball game with the neighborhood high school boys, will show inevitable wear over time. This

usually manifests itself in the form of squeaks, and in the time of the middle of the night when you are trying to sneak into the bathroom looking for four Advil to take care of your knee pain. You may already know the standard American method for getting rid of squeaks, which is to use half a can of WD-40 while doing the indecisive Door Dance: open, close, spray, open, close, spray, open, close on your foot, curse, until realizing that the squeak is not coming from the door, but from the floorboard every time you shift your weight when closing the door. I'd like to offer a better method of fixing an (actual) door squeak.

1) Remove each hinge pin separately.
2) Coat the pin with petroleum jelly, just as you realize that sudden smell of eucalyptus means it wasn't petroleum jelly you grabbed out of the medicine cabinet but Vicks VapoRub.
3) Ask your wife if you have any petroleum jelly.
4) Find the only jar of petroleum jelly you have, which is buried in the back of the bathroom closet because the last time you used it was on your now-teenager's red butt when he or she was a baby.
5) Coat the pin with petroleum jelly.
6) Drop the now slippery pin onto the floor.
7) Pick up the pin, which is now coated with dog fur and a dust bunny that could win a prize at the county fair, and wipe it off.
8) Repeat steps 5-7 until you feel like that episode of <u>Star Trek: The Next Generation</u> where they got stuck in that time loop and keep dying over and over until Ryker knocks the VapoRub out of Data's hand and says: "The squeak is in the

floor, you idiot!"

Floor Squeaks

If you want a sure-fire way to involuntarily get to visit a psychiatrist, or if you've just always wanted to experience what a straight jacket feels like, try fixing a floor squeak. These elusive noises usually occur in high-traffic areas such as the space in front of your couch where you get up to get your snacks during commercials. As annoying as they are, floor squeaks are fixable with the right tools and know how. Here's hoping you somehow find both.

Floor squeaks are usually caused by either the floorboards or floor sheets rubbing against each other, kind of like when you were on vacation as a kid and you and your brother were in the back of a car driving through Nebraska for twelve hours. If you have an unfinished basement with open joists, have a friend stand on the squeak above you while you try to locate the source from below. Now that you've identified the squeaky area, just... wow; sorry — I just couldn't believe you actually found someone to stand on your floor and squeak it for you. Most people have better things to do. Anyway, if you've located the squeak, you can attempt to fix it by using an official floor-squeak-reduction device made by Americans who really wanted to invent something, and a floor squeak reducer was about all that was left uninvented. One of these products, called a "Squeak Ender," attaches to the subfloor and draws it tight to the joist, creating a new, secure floor bond that then causes the squeak to pop up elsewhere. Another method involves pounding a shim between the subfloor and the joist, thus putting pressure on the subfloor to straighten up, or you'll call its parents and have it expelled; you really mean it this time. If you have access to the bare floor, such as after a fire or because you're getting new carpet because you burned a hole in the old carpet accidentally testing a homemade bottle rocket, which would have been really cool, had it worked, you can drill screws from the top down into the joists in order to eliminate the squeak. A final method involves filling the gaps between the joists with construction adhesive, which will either eliminate the squeak, or glue it permanently into your eternal living existence.

After all this, if the squeak still persists, congratulations! You have a mouse. See Chapter 30: "No, Sweetheart, I'm Not Killing Mickey, It's Vermin."

Project: Drywall Repair

REMEMBER THE TIME THAT YOU AND YOUR BROTHERS hung that chin-up bar in the hall closet when your parents were away, but instead of doing chin-ups in it you thought, "Let's take that old tire tube from my bike and sling both ends through the bar, and then use it like a sling shot and see how far we can shoot Mindy's Teddy Ruxpin down the hall," and just as you had stretched the tube way past what your brother was able to do, and you knew this was going to be the winner, the bar shot out of the door frame, whizzed past your head, your brother's head, shot through the bathroom door, and impaled itself in the opposite wall? That would have been a good time to know how to patch a drywall hole, if you hadn't already been grounded for two weeks.

Drywall repairs are common, especially if you live in a home with people, because sooner or later, someone is going to get angry. Usually this involves slamming doors that are not meant to be slammed in that way, and the result is a doorknob-sized hole in your wall. This repair can be easily made once, like everything else in life, except maybe marriage, you know how. With a little patience, some joint compound, and the loss of teenaged cell phone privileges, your wall will be ready for your next failed impromptu anger-management session.

Recommended Tools:
- Hammer
- Accidental hole
- Utility knife or drywall saw
- Drywall compound
- Okay, some extra drywall compound to replace the drywall compound that just fell behind the drywall when you squished it into the hole
- Straightedge (e.g., metal ruler, the cover to this book, kindle reader, etc.)
- Pencil
- Okay, pencil with actual sharpened point
- Pencil with newly sharpened point to replace the previous sharpened pencil whose tip just broke the first time you used it
- 1 x 4 (or 19 mm × 89 mm if you're British or me in math class in the 70s) backer boards
- Drywall screws
- Something that screws in drywall screws
- Drywall scrap leftover from a previous anger-hole repair big enough to cover the current anger hole
- Taping knife (this is not just a knife with tape on it)
- Drywall tape (no, you can't just use masking tape)

1) First, draw a square, rectangle, rhombus or dodecahedron around the aforementioned hole with your straightedge and pencil.
2) Go sharpen your pencil, which just broke again.
3) Make sure the area you are going to cut and remove does not contain any vital organs such

as electrical wires, water pipes, or the pancreas.
4) Make a shallow cut with your utility knife, which is probably the only kind you can make because you're too cheap to put a new blade in it.
5) Keep on making shallow cuts until you give in and decide to put in a new blade.
6) Open the utility knife storage compartment to discover that you are not only so cheap that you don't ever change the blade, but you've never even bought any new blades.
7) Okay, let's try that drywall saw thingy. It's a little more fun, anyway.
8) Cut out the hole you marked with your broken-tipped pencil.
9) If your hole is large, which, judging by the anger levels of most door-slamming teenagers, it is, you'll need to use backer boards inserted behind the hole to brace the patched area.
10) Use drywall screws to secure the backer boards behind the patched area
11) Wow, we're already to 11 and we haven't even slopped any patching stuff in the hole yet. Maybe you should just call a professional.
12) No! We're going to finish what we've started! Now, using the soundtrack from your <u>Rocky IV</u> cassette for inspiration, cut your drywall scrap to fit the current hole, leaving just enough gap to make sure you'll need to cut it again.
13) Secure the drywall patch to the backer boards with those drywall screws you forgot to get more of from the basement in step 10.
14) Remove the drywall patch yet again when you realize you used 1/2" drywall to patch a 3/4"

wall. Re-patch with the correct size, then flip your <u>Rocky IV</u> cassette over, go to track 10 (Training Montage) and turn the volume of your boom box to 9.
15) Ignoring the grimaces and rolled eyes of any nearby teenagers, press a thick layer of drywall compound over the tape with the taping knife you had to borrow from your friend Rick because you didn't know what one was. Do this until the seams around your patch are invisible, like the respect from your wife's eyes when she walks past you with the laundry basket while shaking her head.
16) There are second and third coats that need to be done, so you might want to break out your old Survivor: "Caught in the Game" cassette as well. If you're in a pinch, you can use Asia's "Astra" album.
17) Once everything has dried, sand what will probably be significant, Everest-like bumps out of the patch, and then finally apply the primer and finish coats of paint.

All that's left now is to settle in and wait for the next door slam, which, judging by the mess on the floor you now need to clean up, might be yours.

PART FIVE: OUTDOOR PROJECTS
At Least You Can't Ruin The Carpet Out Here

Tip Time: Renting Tools

SOME PROJECTS WILL REQUIRE more tool power than what you currently have in your arsenal, which means it's time to head to the Home Improvement Warehouse to buy more tools! [Wife: No, it's not.] Okay, then it's time to head to the local tool rental emporium, where your grizzled tool rental employee is ready to snort at you in disgust because you don't know what a "harmonic ridge reamer" is, much less where to put it once it's turned on, much less how to even turn it on. Or where to plug it in. Or that it runs on gas.

Spending money on a tool rental for a home improvement project may seem counterintuitive; do-it-yourself projects are supposed to <u>save</u> money, after all, but keep in mind that it's not every day you can manufacture an excuse to run a machine capable of not only grinding a tree stump to powder, but impressing your neighbor as well, up until the point you accidentally grind through the underground electrical lines that power his house. Here are some examples of common tool rentals and their inherent comical risks.

Power Post Hole Digger
If you need to put in a fence and you don't have a teenage son who needs to raise money for his soccer

team's trip to Panama so they can have a losing season internationally, you should consider renting a power post hole digger. In addition to making quick work out of digging multiple holes, they also have the advantage of looking like something a muscular super villain would use to plant a nuclear weapon into the floor of the Federal Reserve. The two-man auger is the more common version of this tool, with the main feature being the ability to twirl two grown men around like the Tasmanian Devil on Adderall when hitting hard clay. You should consider renting the wheeled, one-man version, which, in addition to being stable, has the added asset of being able to crush your toe. If the surface you are drilling on is flat, figure on being able to drill eight holes per hour. If it is sloped, figure on ultimately paying for a new door for your neighbor's Taurus.

Boom Lift
This is the ultimate dream machine in the male testosterone amplifying tool kit. If male peacocks did yard work to impress other males, they would be floating around in boom lifts, squawking at the entire neighborhood. Not only does it have the word "boom" in it, it also allows you to work with hydraulics and operate levers as if you were a skilled extra in an episode of <u>Emergency</u>, preferably not the one where the guy gets fried in the electrical lines. Boom lifts are those lifting buckets you see the electric company guys lounging in on the side of the road, and are most useful when you need to reach the upper part of a tree for trimming, side of the house for painting, or roof for retrieving your buddy who got thrown up there when you were operating the power post hole digger.

It's much safer than a ladder, even though your wife will be constantly double-checking your will to see if everything is in order while you're operating it. A typical boom can pivot 360 degrees and lift you up to 35 feet in the air, which you've totally just ignored because you were already thinking about all the cool things you could do with this lift already, weren't you? As with most power tools, the boom lift is not a toy, although, man, it sure should be. I mean, if they had these things at Disney and you could have gladiator fights on them, they could totally charge a hundred bucks for twenty minutes. You'll need a truck to haul this around your yard, so, if you don't own one, remember that you can't borrow your buddy Ted's after that toilet disposal debacle, so you'll need to cozy up to someone else at work.

Paint Sprayers
If you have large surfaces to paint such as fences, siding, or plywood sheets, or if you just have a lot of clothes you don't really like any more, consider renting a paint sprayer. These handy tools can cover large surfaces with paint without leaving brush or roller overlap marks, or sometimes any sense that a skilled laborer was involved in the project. A commercial sprayer will take a little practice getting used to, as your only previous experience with spray painting was painting your Pinewood Derby car red with your dad, which brings back bad memories, because you not only ruined his favorite tie, you lost the race to a girl. You can paint a whole room in an hour – even less if the hose breaks – and have enough time left over to adequately explain to the rental company why there is an outline on the side of the

machine in the shape of an angry running cat.

Skid Steer Loader
This powerful machine will make you think you're on a work site with real, sweating construction guys, half of whom are actually working. The skid steer loader is not only a mediocre country band name; it can move gravel, rock, dirt, and the occasional lethargic teenager quickly and easily. Use it when you realize that the area you were going to dig to put in a concrete slab to hold the concrete bags for your next project is not only almost metaphysically redundant, but it is going to take a lot longer than you thought. A skid steer loader can move about 6 dump-truck loads of material a day – even more if your dump trucks are smaller than normal. And, with its powerful, pivoting spinning wheels, you'll soon be ready for your next project: sod replacement. One note, from personal experience: when backing up, avoid making "beep beep beep" noises with your wife present, as she may think you are making a comment about her weight.

Project: Putting in a New Mailbox

REMEMBER IN HIGH SCHOOL when you and your buddies would get into your buddy Russ's Dodge Dart which he nicknamed "Richard the Deep Breather" and go down country roads and each take turns with a baseball bat smacking farmers' mailboxes into left field? Now, remember that noise you heard in the middle of the night last week that sounded like a cheap high school car with half a muffler, some whooping teenaged boys, and a baseball bat hitting something helpless and metallic? Remember how fun life <u>used</u> to be? Remember where your toolbox is?

<u>Recommended Tools:</u>
- Hammer
- Post hole digger, also known as a "clamshell digger," also known as a "heart attack instigator"
- Long 2 x 4 with extra splinters
- Shovel with the mud still caked on it from last fall when the downspout backed up and flooded your kids' playground
- Smaller shovel for getting the caked mud off the larger shovel
- Reciprocating saw, because you just never know

- Level
- Another level to make sure the first level is really level, because it was your dad's and your remember him using it to pound in tent stakes
- Okay, just buy a post level which measures two sides of the post at the same time
- New mailbox, or just an old shoebox and some bungee cords if you're in a hurry

A new mailbox is a great "curb appeal" project, which means anyone driving by your house will think what a classy person you are, even though they have no idea who you are and you'll never meet them again in your entire life. But, let's see if we can try to impress them anyway.

1) First, we'll need to dig a hole for the mailbox post, which, if you've never done it before, is some of the more strenuous work you can undertake, up there with doing taxes or going shopping. Using the post hole digger you borrowed from your neighbor Ed, who didn't tell you that he replaced the broken rivets holding the left blade on with two paper clips, begin digging your new hole. Make sure that the paper clip/rivets shear off after two plunges into your hard, clay dirt, slicing off the big toe of your new boots and nearly bisecting your big toe.

2) Next, after spending two hours replacing the missing rivets with a bolt salvaged from your lawn mower because it was the only size you could find that fit, complete the digging of the hole, right up to the part where you sever your

cable TV line because you forgot to call 811. Now, with your pre-teenage daughter swarming all over you like a possessed bee because she was in the middle of an extremely important <u>Pretty Little Liars</u> episode she'd only seen two times before, temporally splice the broken cable with some electrical tape and leftover electronic bits you still have from when you set up your grandmother's Magnavox TV in 1982, then wait for the cable company to arrive on Monday because it's a weekend.

3) In the meantime, finish digging your hole, up until the point where you hit a tree root, which, no matter how many times you attempt to remove it with whacks from your increasingly dull post hole digger, as well as the use of your extensive and loud PG-13 vocabulary words, you realize that there is a reciprocating saw in the tools listed above. Using the saw and a long, coarse blade, cut the tree root at each edge of the hole, making sure to make one last cut to just clean it up a little, and thereby nick the splice you just made in the cable TV line.

4) Once you've reached your desired depth, which you'll know because you don't think you can dig any more without provoking an aneurysm, use your 2 x 4, or, alternatively, a 4 x 2, and tamp down the dirt at the base of the hole. This not only helps prevent the post from settling, but more importantly, provides you with some much-needed aggression release. This is also a good time to tell you that you could have used a power post hole digger (See previous chapter), but since you seem to be turning red, maybe I

shouldn't have brought it up.
5) Position the post in the hole, then use your level to make sure it is setting perpendicular. Clumsily fill the dirt back into the hole by kicking it with your shoe because, for crying out loud, you can't hold the level and the post and a shovel all at the same time. Remember that the universe exists in three dimensions, which means you'll need to check to see if all sides of your post are vertically level, or your new mailbox may learn forward threateningly, and potentially frighten your mail delivery person.
6) Tamp the dirt with your 2 x 4 (or 4 x 2) until the hole is filled, the post is sturdy and straight, and you realize you can't find your favorite screwdriver, which is now buried securely at the bottom of your new hole, waiting for some space-age suburban archeologist to discover it in 2000 years, laugh uproariously, and provide you with some bonus, eon-spanning, do-it-yourself embarrassment.
7) Now that your post is in securely, you can attach your mailbox, because your mail carrier person has been impatiently waiting in his or her little mail truck for the last 20 minutes for you to finish this project. Many modern mailboxes are made of vinyl, which has the advantage of being more weather- and Louisville Slugger-immune than metal. Make sure you get one with the red flag you can flip up on the side so your mail person knows when you're ready to mail the emergency room bill from your last project.

8) Using your cordless drill with the half-dead battery, attach the mailbox by inserting the screws approximately halfway before the drill grinds to a halt, then, still pressing on the switch, try to use the drill like a screwdriver by twisting it. After realizing this never works, pick up a screwdriver and finish the job, repeating the same tedious process for all of the other screws.

You are now ready to receive mail in style and class; however, you might want to keep your shotgun handy in case those teenagers show up again tonight.

Project: Building a Wooden Fence

PUTTING IN A FENCE IS A LOT OF WORK that involves holes, possible Advil addiction, and potential years of crookedness (I meant the fence but possibly you as well). I put it in here because I did it once, and I didn't want to feel like the only one who's set four posts in the ground before realizing he had been using the post level upside down. Note: putting in a fence is a multi-day project, and may take longer than you think, just like that time you figured it would take an afternoon to put up a window box, then realized, pretty much right about the time you smashed the window when the ladder slipped, that it was going to take longer than you thought. But, for those of you who desperately desire to fence out your neighbor Chet, who is addicted to Little Debby Cosmic Brownies, and likes to sun his puffy, oily body on his yellow plastic chaise lounge every Saturday because he read somewhere that Vitamin D can decrease hair loss, here are some tips.

Recommended Tools:
- Hammer
- Post level
- The guy at Lowe's to tell you what a "post level" is

- The phone number for the guy at Lowe's so you can ask him how you're supposed to use the post level you just bought from him
- Bucket with wire handle that cuts into your hand when it gets heavy
- Wheelbarrow (preferably not the one with the flat tire that you haven't fixed yet because it was winter and the garage was "too cold")
- Posthole digger you borrowed from your neighbor Carl who's still waiting for you to return his orbital sander
- The phone number for the guy at Lowe's you got the post level from so you can ask him how you're supposed to use the post hole digger
- Lowe's gift card for the guy at Lowe's because he promised not to tell anyone why you keep calling
- Caulk gun
- Shovel
- String line
- Cement trowel, or, in a pinch, your wife's pie spatula

Choosing the Right Height

Your first step in planning your new fence is to determine the height. A few important factors will help you make your decision. If your yard slopes down into your neighbor's, you may be able to get by with a shorter fence, some well-placed shrubbery, or, if you live in the rural south, a row of rusty appliances. If you are trying to screen yourself from your neighbors (or vice versa: see Chet, above), you may need a taller fence, which means more materials, which means more money, which means no new 56" TV to watch the All-Star Game on when this project is finally over.

One way to determine how tall your fence needs to be is to take a piece of cardboard from the ping pong table box you somehow managed to assemble at Christmas, cut it to the proposed height of the fence, and have a helper walk to different positions around your yard while you observe from your back door to see if the suggested height is going to be sufficient for blocking Chet. Painting a helpful message on the cardboard, such as "Hey - we're thinking about building a fence but it's nothing personal, really (Hi Chet)" may help diffuse any future neighborly squabbles.

Make sure to determine the spacing of your fence posts before you start, because once you've spent an hour digging through rock-hard clay for just one post, you'll be tempted to space your posts about, say, every 20 feet, and maybe even decide to just let the bottom of the fence rest on the ground. Remember, if your posts are spaced too far apart you run the risk of what is know in Home Improvement circles as "fence sag"; an embarrassing condition which can only be remedied by a humiliating visit from "Verne's Fence Fixing Service For Lazy Guys Who Haven't Worked Out Since They Were On The Tennis Team in High School." You also may find yourself, after having what must certainly have been a raging heart attack putting in just four or five posts, suddenly trying to convince your spouse that installing more of a "privacy screen" as opposed to an entire freaking fence around the yard is a better idea, and you also just now remembered you saw it on Pinterest and quite possibly <u>The Today</u>

Show with that one lady with the short hair she likes.

Installing the Actual Fence Part
Next, you need to attach upper and lower, and, in extreme cases (see "fence sag," above), middle rails to your fence posts, which provide the support for the boards that will do the actual fence action of this project. The best part about this stage of the project is you get to use "butt joints," which allow for the giggling of grown men as they act like they're still in junior high. Next, attach your vertical fence boards. If you prefer more junior high giggling, you can use "half blind, half lap" or "doweled butt" joints here, but it's probably not worth all that extra work just for the laughs. Use a string line, which is essentially a line of string, along the top of the boards to keep them level. Or just nail them all up and saw off the tops later; I don't care. About every tenth board, check the sports scores to make sure this interminable project hasn't spilled over from baseball spring training and now, holy smokes, the Rose Bowl is next week.

Planting a Post That Doesn't Rot
A common problem for fence posts is that they, like the original copy of The Declaration of Independence, or Hostess Twinkies, are susceptible to rot when exposed to moisture over time. There is a simple solution to this, however, which is to not build a fence. But, since you've probably already dug the holes, here are some suggestions.
1) Try soaking the bottom of the posts in a wood preserver, such as copper naphthenate, which is probably the same thing the Germans used in World War I as chemical warfare, but will keep

moisture from invading the base of the post.
2) Put about 5-6 inches of aggregate in the bottom of the post hole. If you don't know what aggregate is, it's gravel, but I guess the bigwigs who went to Home Improvement College have to justify their student loans, so they call it "aggregate." Anyway, the "aggregate" will help prevent moisture from collecting at the bottom of the hole, as it is apparently equipped with tiny police batons and bullhorns.
3) Once the concrete around the post has cured, apply some acrylic caulk to the gaps between the concrete and the post. This keeps moisture out, and also gives you an excuse to use that new caulking gun you bought on eBay that looks like a Star Trek hand phaser (TOS).
4) Put down your smart phone and stop searching for "Star Trek caulking gun"; I just made that up.

There you go! Now you can exist in a bare-Chetless universe, free from embarrassment, except for that nagging case of fence sag you can't seem to get rid of, no matter how much aggregate you take.

Tip Time: Freeing Stuck Nuts, Bolts and Screws

ANY TIME YOU'RE WORKING ON an older object, such as the 1970s-vintage lawn mower you inherited from your dad that you refuse to get rid of because it's the only thing that can mow the scrub brush in the far back yard without coughing up blood, you may come across a nut or bolt that refuses to budge, no matter how many curse words it hears. Here are a few tips to help you loosen even the most stubborn of nuts, bolts, screws, or those things with the round tops that look like acorns I can never remember the name of.

Loosening Nuts and Bolts
1) Try tightening the nut first. This may loosen the nut for removal, or just show you that you forgot that old handyman adage: lefty-loosey, whitey-tighty... wait, loosey goosey — loosey-tighty, whitey-flighty... okay, I obviously can't remember it either; just bang on it until it moves one way or the other.
2) Try tapping the nut with a hammer as a reminder that you have other, heavier tools available, and it might want to consider loosening before someone gets hurt.
3) Apply heat to the nut, which may loosen it, because Physics says so. This also has the

added advantage of being able to play with fire, but the admitted disadvantage of potentially starting an inconvenient gas fire in your garage.
4) Use a chemical such as Liquid Wrench, Big Wet Mallet, or *&^%$#!! You Better Loosen Up! and soak the joint thoroughly. Be sure to try this <u>after</u> trying option 3, because, again, inconvenient gas fire/garage/etc.
5) Try using an impact driver to loosen the nut. These are those cool tools you hear about all the time in the tire-changing garages that make you sound like you're on Richard Petty's pit crew at the Daytona 500. For smaller nuts and bolts (your daughter's bike she left out in the rain, the wheelbarrow you left out in the rain, etc.) you can use a set of high-end, hex-shaft nut drivers, that is, if you can avoid laughing long enough because you just read "nut drivers." Grow up. For larger nuts (car tires, space shuttles, Mechagodzilla left out in the rain), get some six-point, impact-rated, black finish sockets. The six points keep the socket from stripping, and the black finish just looks really boss on your workbench when you're trying to impress your father-in-law. If you don't have access to an impact driver, you can use a breaker bar, which is a long socket wrench that gives the extra leverage you need to really injure your knee when it slips.
6) If your nut refuses all of these attempts, it is probably 5 o'clock and time to call it a day and see if Menard's is having a sale on lawn mowers.

Loosening Screws

If the slot on a screw head is mangled beyond description because you used the wrong size of screwdriver again, don't worry; you can probably just buy a new one of whatever it is that's busted. But if you really need to remove the screw because it's, say, keeping your wife from mowing the lawn, here are the tips.

1) Using the blade of your hacksaw (you do have a hacksaw, don't you? Didn't you use it last summer to cut the pipe on your kid's swing set so you could save the bird they said fell inside the slide, only to find the bird was really a plastic dinosaur?), cut a new slot in the head of the screw, making sure to scratch whatever paint around the screw will be the most noticeable.

2) File the edges of two sides of the screw so you can slip your adjustable wrench around it, crank too hard on it, and now completely strip the head off.

3) Try using a screw extractor, a fluted, horror-movie-looking device made of hardened steel that you drill into the center of the screw counter clockwise (for those of you with digital watches, good luck), thus drawing out the screw. Because the bit is made from very hard, brittle steel, be sure to apply too much torque on the extractor, thereby breaking it off in the screw, allowing you an excuse to finally buy that new snow blower you've always wanted.

Project: Cutting Down a Tree

THERE WAS A TIME, when people didn't have time for such a thing as "home improvement" because they were too busy trying not let winter kill them, that an average man could chop down a tree, remove the bark, whittle it down to a pipe, and smoke it before breakfast. Since I'm going to assume that you, like me, do not smoke a pipe, we're going to try an easier way.

Recommended Tools:
- Hammer
- 5 or 6 concurrently stacked hard hats
- Chain saw (e.g., that thing with the whirling blade that your wife thinks you are going to cut your foot off with even before you start it)
- Earmuffs (the non-fuzzy kind)
- Safety glasses (not just your bifocals)
- Hard hat (not just your high school football helmet)
- Kevlar chaps, which is not an unfortunate skin condition but protective pants for your legs
- Bold sense of adventure

Downing a tree is one of the most dangerous things a home handyman will ever undertake, along with trying to convince your wife that an A-Teamthemed bathroom complete with talking B.A. Baracus toilet ("I pity the poo!") will actually increase the value of your house. If you are in doubt about your tree toppling skills, and you should be, you should seriously consider getting a professional, or just letting gravity eventually do its job. However, in some cases, trees are either dead or dying, and in danger of falling and damaging property, or just plain begging for you to try out the new chain saw you got for Christmas.

1) To get started, you need to estimate the "felling zone," which is the area that you will get crushed in unless you're not in it when the aforementioned gravity part happens. Remember, just like the size of that guy who gets out of his Prius after you honk at him because he didn't move fast enough after the light turned green, trees are taller than you think. You can estimate tree height by using the "ax handle method," where you take your ax handle, hold it straight out at arms length, and wave it a little to attract your neighbor's attention so you can ask him if you can borrow his cool laser rangefinder. Once you have determined your tree's height, always give yourself a little extra room, such as by standing in the garage.

2) Plan your escape route carefully, allowing yourself two exit possibilities. You may want to make elaborate charts, graphs, or models like you see used in movies where the thief has to steal the gold using only a Mini Cooper, some candle wax, and a first edition copy of <u>A Tale of</u>

Two Cities. This doesn't really serve any practical purpose, as it is kind of hard to outrun a falling tree once it's started falling, but it may fool your wife into thinking you know what you're doing.
3) Approach the tree with caution, as trees can sense danger and are apt to fall on you just out of self-preservation. You may want to consider talking to the tree in soothing tones, assuring it that the sharp, running chainsaw you are holding in your hands is just there to protect it from other trees, who are mean, but not THIS tree; this tree is a nice tree, etc.
4) Cut down the tree.
5) At this point you should be running very fast, possibly faster than you thought possible, never having been in danger of being crushed by a large object before, unless you count the time your mom told you you had to dance the May Day Dance with Judy Steenger, who was bigger than two girls combined, and she tripped on her dress and pushed you into the folding chairs where all the guys were sitting and it was the first time you were that close to a girl but not the way you had planned. The tree should be falling in the direction you told it to, which should not be in the same direction as your neighbor's new Volvo, or any other valuable object, such as children. Considering the tree is now dead because you just killed it, it may not hear too well, so yelling really won't help.

Once the tree is down, your work is just beginning, as you have about a whole weekend of slicing it up ahead of you, unless your wife is back from shopping and is wondering why her new rose arbor has been crushed by a tree, in which case you should probably hide in the garage for a while, unless you smashed that, too.

Project: Planting a Tree

NOTHING BEAUTIFIES A HOME more than a gorgeous, sturdy tree that the previous homeowner planted long before you showed up. But since you weren't that lucky, it's up to you, your shovel, and that new tree sticking out of your minivan window to make it happen.

Recommended Tools:
- Hammer
- Shovel
- Smaller shovel that you can actually lift dirt with without permanently injuring your groin
- Tarp
- Wheelbarrow

Before starting any project that involves the average guy (you) using a shovel, post hole digger, or really anything bigger than a dull pooper scooper, you need to call 811. This is the number that will, overnight, summon the Multicolored Utility Flag Fairy to plant about 245 little plastic flags in various places on your lawn in secret patterns designed by utility companies, possibly in order to spell derogatory messages about you when seen from by passing satellites. Each color represents a potential way you could really screw things up, from a minor gas leak, sewer eruption, or electrocution, to really serious things such as losing your cable right before the playoffs start.

Choosing a tree is like choosing a mother-in-law; it will most likely be hanging around for decades, in the same place, until you have grandchildren, constantly reminding you whether you did a good job or not, and will secretly think her only daughter should've married Hank Stilton instead, because at least he knows not to plant a tree directly under a power line. Plant a tree according to your "hardiness zone," which is not whether there is a 1/3 Pound Bacon Cheeseburger available in your area, but a geographically defined zone that determines whether that orange tree you planted in your Minneapolis back yard is going to give you juice next spring or just a reason to rent a wood chipper. Also consider the size the tree will be when full-grown when planting near structures, as you don't want the next owner of your house to have to decide whether it would be cool to build a tree house in the maple tree growing through his garage.

1) Dig the hole approximately 1.2 times larger than what your wheelbarrow will carry so that it will be too hard to wheel, causing you to accidentally dump it sideways, spilling half the dirt onto your driveway.
2) Plant your tree so the "root collar," the area on the tree where it would normally wear a bow tie, is about 1 inch above the soil level. If you have your Tree Collar Soil Laser Level, use that; otherwise, just guess like I do.
3) If the tree is planted too shallowly, it will make

poor decisions, and rely on its friends for its self esteem, begin smoking, and eventually marry a used car salesman before blowing over in a storm. But don't plant it too deeply, either, as it will become smug and start listening to music only on vinyl because the quality is SO much better than digital, especially the stuff out of Decca in the 60s.

4) Backfill the tree with the dirt you previously removed, as this is the dirt with which it is most familiar, and Tree Psychologists now agree that this is the best way to help a tree grow up to become a well-adjusted and highly-oxygenated member of society. Soil amendments can discourage the tree from spreading its roots, causing it to want to sit at the nerd table in the lunchroom, where it will be taunted by larger, more muscular trees with flawless bark and who date the cute sapling down the street.

5) Find some of that black plastic corrugated downspout material left over from when you had to divert the rainwater away from the house after that storm caused your downspout to carve a miniature Grand Canyon through your azalea bushes. Taking about a 3-foot section, split it along its length using your utility knife with the old, rusty blade you dulled to butter-knife sharpness when you were using it to open paint cans (see Basic Tools). Fit the plastic around the tree, making sure to pinch your fingers at least three times because you left your gloves in the basement after you were done unplugging the toilet and you may have

gotten some toilet water on them and you're not sure you even want to touch them again. This plastic will help protect the tree from animals, disease, and your weed-whacker-wielding son when he's trying to set the yard record for grass trimming so he can get back inside the house to play more <u>Meta-Death Rezombinizer 5: BRAINZ!</u>. Most importantly, it makes your neighbors think you really know what you're doing with this tree planting stuff.

6) Mulching your tree not only provides protection, insulation, and moisture retention for your new tree, but also a reason to break out the shop vac, as the inevitable broken mulch bag you bought has leaked itself all over the back of your car. I recommend not using plastic or landscape fabric around trees, as these are a real pain to cut into a circle, and your utility knife is dull enough already (again, see Basic Tools).

7) Water your tree often, to the point that you wondered why you even planted this thing in the first place, as it's almost as bad as taking care of a new puppy, except in reverse, where you want the tree to take water, not make it.

Your new tree should establish itself in a few months, and you can take satisfaction in your landscaping accomplishment, until fall, when you realize you forgot that you hate raking leaves.

Project: Pest Protection (No, Sweetheart, I'm Not Killing Mickey, It's Vermin)

WE SHARE THE WORLD with many creatures, many of which seem to want to also share my Cheetos and WiFi, because they keep trying to get inside my house. Here are some suggestions on how to get rid of some of the more common unwanted home invaders, such as bugs, mice, small yippy punting dogs, salesmen, and [Insert Favorite Mother-in-Law Comment Here].

Recommended Tools:
- Hammer
- Old deadly spray stuff in a leaky brown bottle leftover from your dad's garage that looks like it could melt the paint off a Chernobyl fire truck
- Every mousetrap ever invented by man, including the ones that you can't ever tell your children you used or they will never hug you again
- Ant killing bait that looks like Karo syrup but don't try using it in your Scotcheroos or you won't be able to care that you even have ants anymore

Ants

If you are a male, you may not know you even have ants, unless you live with a female, in which case you are probably infested with them. All it takes is the discovery of one lost, little ant with a tiny map looking for the right road back to the ant hill for you to be commanded to wage all-out insect war. Aside from using the sun and a computer-controlled array of insect-sensing magnifying glasses, here are some simple (i.e. "chemically weaponized") ways of controlling (i.e. "completely and forever destroying") these pesky insects. Unless you're dealing with a broken ant farm, in which case, good luck. Experts agree that using ant bait is the best way to annihilate these critters, because the ant does not ingest the poison himself, he carries it back to the nest, much like when you get a Domino's pizza delivery, eat a slice at the door, and take the rest back to your family. If you have carpenter ants, which you'll know because they'll be carrying toolboxes and have bandages on their tiny, calloused fingers, you'll need to call a pro, because they can reduce a house to sawdust in minutes. At least that's what I remember from some old Warner Brothers cartoons.

Spiders, Bugs, Beetles, Cockroaches, Cooties, Millipedes, Centipedes, Monopedes, All The Beasts Of The Earth And All The Birds In The Sky And All The Creatures That Move Along The Ground — Everything That Has The Breath Of Life In It

For your standard wife-screaming-stand-on-the-chair type of bugs, you should try spraying a preventative bug barrier around the outside and inside of your house. This will act like one of those Soviet-era border gates you see in 80s movies, with the annoyed-looking guards who ask you for your papers before squishing you under their boots. Most of these products are colorless and odorless, so expect to see them used in an episode of CSI soon. They can last up to a year, which will allow you more time for taking care of your mouse problem, which is our next section.

Mice
The most shuddersome, the absolute creepiest sound you can ever hear in the middle of the night, next to your dog vomiting on your new carpet, is the sound of a mouse scritching across your ceiling. You may be the biggest animal-lover this side of Snow White; you may have marched 12 miles in the rain in Washington, D.C., to try to save some red-butted baboons in Tangiers, but you would shoot Bambi in the face if it meant that mouse would become instantly and completely dead. (Bonus tip for Floridians and Texans: wherever you see "mouse," insert the word "cockroach.") Fortunately, there are many baits, traps, and devices that can successfully eradicate a mouse and his pals. Unfortunately, some of them are not what I would call humane, but you probably won't care about that right now, because I just saw something small and furry running into your pantry. Snap traps are the most time-honored method of mouse execution, and, although they may seem cruel, they do provide the mouse with a quick and clean death, and you with a body you can do a victory dance over. They will also most likely provide you with a few sore fingers, as setting one of these touchy things is a lesson in trembling, sweaty anxiety. Favorite baits of

professionals for traps are chocolate syrup and peanut butter, or, to save time, just use a Reese's peanut butter cup.

Home Improvement Glossary

Allowable Span
The optimum allowable distance between the time you swung the ladder into the bay window because you tripped on the hose you forgot to put away like your wife said and the time you should attempt to slink back into the house without her noticing.

Ampacity
Refers to the how much current a wire will usually carry through your finger because you switched off the wrong breaker in the breaker box. For example, a 12-gauge electrical copper wire can safely carry up to 20 amps into your shriveling pancreas.

Anchor Bolts
The 'L' shaped bolts that, in retrospect, you should have sunk into the concrete foundation of your new shed as you are now watching it slide into your neighbor's garage.

Architrave
A supervillain featured originally in <u>The Incredible Hulk #43</u>, he was known for committing sprees of diabolical ornamental molding carvings around door or window frames.

Automatic Center Punch
An Ultimate Fighter move in Level 4.

Awl
A southern expression of inclusiveness; e.g., "Awl ya'll shud come on over heah when ah gets more washun machines added to muh porch project."

Backfill
What you do when Phil wants you to confirm to his wife that yes, he did remember to fill up the truck with gas last week and she must have just not noticed it was getting empty.

Backflow
A reverse flow of water or other liquids out of sewer pipes which usually occurs the Saturday your in-laws arrive for a weeklong visit.

Ball Peen Hammer
A cocktail drink made from a 1/2 ounce of Rock and Rye liqueur, 2 jiggers of vodka, and 2 teaspoons of lemon juice.

Baluster
One of the supporting spindles in a handrail used by small children to absolutely scare the bejeebus out of their moms when they try to squeeze through them.

Band Clamp
An immense, rubber clamp used to keep overly boisterous bands from falling off stage.

Band Saw
What the band sees just before falling off stage.

Barge Board
An annoying type of board that always manages to push its way into your conversations.

Belt Sander
An aggressive type of sander fitted with a coarse, abrasive belt used to grind down door edges, uneven doorframes, and the knuckles of your left hand.

Bevel-edge Chisel
A tiny but combative bird mostly found flying around inside of large home improvement stores.

Board and Batten
An upscale clothing chain for big and tall women.

Board Foot
The volume of a piece of lumber equal to 12 inches square and one inch thick. For example, a piece of wood 1/2" thick, 6 inches wide, and 24 inches long is equal to 2 inches short of the board you needed to finish the deck tonight before it started to rain.

Brick Mason's Hammer
In ancient lore, the gilded weapon of Brick Mason, a semi-fictional character from badly named private eye mythology.

Butt Joint
Too easy - no comment.

Cantilever
What you might ask when you wonder why a guy hasn't ditched a manipulative, rude woman.

Cap Flashing
What Captain America was arrested for during a lax in proper behavior.

Caulking
A flexible material used to ruin your best pair of jeans because you were too lazy to put on your work clothes.

C-clamps
What you say to a person who does not believe you own any clamps.

Chamfer
How to ask what a cham is for.

Chatoyance
Getting a text message when you are in an important meeting.

Circular Saw
A popular tool used for accidentally cutting your sawhorses in half.

Chalk Line
The outline used to mark where your body lay after you fell off the roof trying to fix your defective Christmas lights.

Class "A" Fire Resistance
The highest fire-resistance rating for roofing per

ASTM E-108, which you already are familiar with after that visit by the fire department to put out the fire on your shed roof you started when you attached the roman candle to the lawn mower for your impromptu backyard 4th of July parade.

Closed Cut Valley
In roofing, this is a valley treatment in which you install shingles from one side of the valley to extend across the valley, while shingles from the other side are trimmed 2 inches from the valley centerline, just before you call the professional roofer to come and do it right.

Closet Bolts
A type of fastening rod that always dreamed of being a screw, but its parents made it go to bolt school.

Code
National, state, and local regulations that govern materials and building techniques for you to find out about after your project is done and your smart neighbor Earl says, "Is that thing to code?"

Cold Chisel
(Slang) A raw deal: "That was one cold chisel, man."

Compound Miter Saw
Used to make compound-angle miter cuts on things such as moldings and door trim over and over until you give up from frustration because they never fit right.

Continuity Tester
The electrical tool your emergency room doctor is telling you to buy before you try installing another dimmer switch.

Coping Saw
A narrow, metal framed saw with a thin blade that snaps every time you try to fix the bad miter cuts you made with your compound miter saw.

Cordless Drill
Just like a corded drill, except you can drop it a lot farther.

Cranked-neck Rasp
A long-legged waterfowl with a sharp beak used for carving concave shapes out of wood.

Curved-tooth File
This prehistoric fish dined exclusively on crank-necked rasps during the late Cretaceous period.

Drill Press
Developed by Bobby Knight at Indiana University, the Drill Press was useful for punching holes in players' self-esteems.

Electronic Studfinder
An essential tool for locating the correct place to drill through your water pipe because you forgot to change the stupid battery again.

English Bow Saw
Just like an American bow saw except it says "lift"

instead of "elevator."

Japanese Panel Saw
A professional wrestling move popularized by Tojo Yamamoto in the 1970s, which involved a Japanese arm drag with an inverted atomic drop, followed by a cobra clutch driver into a double leg flapjack into a pit of vipers.

Laser Plumb Bob
A modern version of the traditional plumb bob, with the added feature of being able to burn your eye out with a laser.

Machinist's Vise
A spinoff of the popular Miami Vice television show, this show mostly just featured a bunch of greasy guys sitting around smoking and talking about NASCAR.

Magnetic-tip Screwdriver
A screwdriver with a magnetic tip that assists you in picking up paper clips, iron filings, tiny sharp tacks – pretty much everything except screws.

Nail Puller
A V-notch in this tool slips under the nail head while a long handle provides extra leverage to pull up that nail you just pounded into the wrong board.

Nail Sets
Use these when you want to unintentionally add many decorative extra holes around the nail heads you are trying to sink below the surface of your project.

Orbital Sander
Launched in May of 2001, this probe is expected to sand smooth the rings of Saturn by the year 2020.

Parapet
The difficult balance beam skill that secured the overall gymnastics gold medal for Nadia Comaneci in the 1976 Olympics.

Pneumatic Nailer
Perfect for quickly power-driving nails through framing 2 x 4s and into your best friend's foot.

Pry Bar
An unpopular type of drinking establishment where wives are allowed to come and ask their husbands why they haven't finished installing that new mirror in the bathroom yet.

Rabbet Plane
A plane with a wide blade ideal for trimming dadoes, rabbets, moles, voles, jerboas, parsnips, and turlingdromes.

Reciprocating Saw
An indispensable saw for remodelers, it can cut through wood, metal, plastics, and the back side of your new kitchen cabinets by way of your bathroom-remodeling job with ease.

Rip Hammer
The son of Rip Torn, know mostly for his role in <u>Men in Black III</u>, where he was the voice of one of those worm guys.

Rifflers
Gangs of mostly harmless thugs who wander empty construction sites looking for riffles.

Router
When fitted with a myriad of useful bits, this tool is capable of leaving a lot of sawdust on the floor for you to track into the kitchen and get yelled at for.

Sabre Saw
Your best bet when you need to cut curved lines, holes, or the cord to the tool you forgot was right under your project.

Speed Square
One of the most popular and useful tools for carpentry, which no one has ever been able to figure out because of all the numbers printed on it.

Square File
For use after forgetting the round hole you just made was supposed to be square.

Torpedo Level
A small but powerful device used by Japanese mini subs in World War II to straighten pictures of Emperor Hirohito on their walls.

Trammel Points
Points you get for knowing that Alan Trammel was not only the Detroit Tigers' shortstop but also manager from 2003-2005.

Two-handed Screwdriver
Features a unique double-grip handle that allows you to dig holes for tulip bulbs twice as fast because you're too lazy to find your bulb planter.

Warrington Hammer
An essential for woodworkers, it features a cross-peen bi-cropped parlimentary-procedured pivot flange, allowing for more finely crafted mini-coopering of barrel bolsters, cruck mongers, and cuttlefish.

Wet Saw
What you get when you drop your sabre saw from your extension ladder into your hot tub because you thought a wasp landed on your hand.

Home Improvement Haikus

Yes, I heard it pop!
What; you think I'm a moron?
Just don't answer that

No, not CFL
I'd actually like to see
Before I get there

Red wire or black wire?
That's one more little lesson
I'll never forget

Turn it off turn it
Off turn it off turn it off
Turn it off thank you

What was it again?
Lefty loosey righty tight?
Then why won't it move?!

My dad was so right
Spackle is the antidote
For angry door knobs

I see it *now*, but
It'd be more helpful if you'd
Just get the wet vac

Pop, fizz, pop, pop, spark
Sizzle, pop, spark spark spark poof
I hate everything

If the devil had
A wrench that twisted your soul
It would be metric

Epilogue

"Hello, Home Help Hotline. My name is Janice; how can I help?"

"Um, yeah, um… is there, like, a guy I can talk to there?"

"I'm sorry, sir?"

"Is there a man there I can talk to?"

"I'm sorry, sir, I'm the only one on duty at the moment."

"Okay, sure, well…"

"I'm sure I can help you, sir; what seems to be the problem?"

"Well, nothing major really, I should probably…"

"Wait, is that you, Kevin?"

"Oh, hi, yeah it's me again."

"Hi, Kevin, what seems to be the problem this week?"

"Um, well, I just got back from having to go shopping, and we were at the mall and I got lost looking for my wife in a Bath & Body Works, and I must have still been a little dazed from the smell, so, I uh…"

Pause.

"Are you still there, Kevin?"

(Female voice in background: "Just tell her!")

"Right, so when I got home I decided to put up

some of those wire shelves in the garage because my wife, she kept tripping over the Christmas light boxes that were by this old pile of patio bricks which I was using to prop up the picnic table I keep meaning to finish but it's holding up the broken..."

"Kevin, are you injured?"

"You know that tool they use to tighten the bolts on, um...?"

"A dog leg mortar hawk with a flange breaker?"

"Yeah... how did you —"

"I'm a professional, Kevin. Go on."

"Okay, so I was ready to attach the braces for the wire shelves into the wall studs like I thought the instructions said, but they were mostly in Chinglish, so what I thought was 'staple' must really have been 'stable' or something because right after that the, um, thing happened."

"Kevin, if you're injured you should probably go to the ER and have them check you out."

"Well, normally I would, but you know when I was there last week to get my arm re-casted after the roof snowblower thing —"

"Roof snowblower?"

"— they said if I showed up there this week they were going to staple my thumbs together so I couldn't do any more harm to myself. I think they were kidding but the lady there looked pretty serious and she was big and had a tattoo of, like, a shark with a machine gun or something —"

"Ok, Kevin, so do you need medical attention?"

"Well, it's pretty ironic, really; I think the word is ironic. Or maybe it's sarcasm..."

"What is?"

"Is ironic like when you are just talking about

something bad happening to someone and you laugh and then the something bad actually happens to the someone, but you don't really laugh then because it's you?"

"I'm... not sure. Maybe you mean..."

"Well, I ran out of nails so I thought I'd use the staple gun and... well, I stapled my thumbs together."

(Unintelligible; possible snickering)

"So you're calling me on the phone with your thumbs stapled together?"

"Yeah; actually my wife makes me keep this number on speed dial so I was able to use the voice activation thing —"

"Okay, Kevin —"

"Normally you'd think it would hurt, something like stapling your thumbs together, but it's not that bad, at least not nearly as bad as my leg."

"Your leg? What happened to your leg?"

"Well, when I stapled my thumbs together I couldn't really hold on to the ladder anymore and I kind of fell onto the lawn mower."

"Kevin, I'm sending an ambulance to your house right now."

"Oh, no, don't worry about it, my wife already did that right after I threw up."

(sound of distant sirens)

"You threw up? What hap —"

"Yeah; I guess when I hit my arm on the stack of patio bricks after bouncing off the lawn mower I twisted my ankle just enough to smack my head on the snow blower. You know, I should really finish that patio. Anyway, she just wanted me too let you know. Again."

(sound of men talking)

"Kevin, is the ambulance there?"

"Oh yeah, they've got the stretcher thing just like last time. Hi Bob. Yeah, staples! Pretty cool, huh?"

"Kevin? Are you still there?"

(voices fading)

"Hey, do any of you guys speak Chinglish? Tell me that doesn't say 'staple'".

Thanks for reading!

Word-of-mouth is crucial for authors to succeed. I'd be extremely grateful if you'd help me inflict further books and columns on humanity by doing one of the following:

- Consider posting a brief review at your favorite ebook site. It makes a big difference!
- Sign up for my mailing list at danvanoss.com and get notified about new books, free books, and specials.
- Tell your friends on Facebook and Twitter.

Want more?

Check out my weekly humor column at the Dubious Knowledge Institute on my author site, danvanoss.com.

Hashtag your Myface here:

Twitter: @dubiouski
Facebook: https://www.facebook.com/dubiouski
Website: danvanoss.com

Coming next:

Sports Survival Guide for Men
Dubious Knowledge (Book Two)
Get notified before anyone else when they are available by signing up at danvanoss.com.

About the author
Dan Van Oss grew up reading just about everything he could borrow from the town library, although admittedly sometimes just to get the sticker segments so he could complete the Reading Centipede for each book he finished. He's had pieces published on humorwriters.org, won second place in the Mona Schreiber Prize for Humorous Fiction and Nonfiction, was a semi-finalist in the humorpress.com writing contest, and was mentioned honorably in the Soul-Making Keats Literary Competition for Humor. He's a

Midwest guy, having spent time in Michigan and Kentucky, but mostly Iowa, where he now lives. He started writing during college, where he enjoyed getting red lines drawn through his Creative Writing projects, and where he also penned a weekly column in the school paper under the pseudonym "Fletcher Ford". He's currently working on his *Survival Guide for Men* series, which will include books on Home Improvement and Sports. You can catch his weekly humor column, the "Dubious Knowledge Institute," at his author site, danvanoss.com. He also plays piano, Hammond organ and anything else with keys; you can check out some of his songs and recordings at Reverbnation.com.

To my grandfathers, who climbed ladders, painted houses, built bird houses and benches, all before there were lithium batteries or conveniently located emergency rooms.

Printed in Great Britain
by Amazon